THE BEATLES

Published in 2020 by Welbeck

An Imprint of Welbeck Non-Fiction Limited, part of Welbeck Publishing Group.

20 Mortimer Street London W1T 3JW

Design copyright © 2020 Welbeck Non-Fiction Limited, part of Welbeck Publishing Group

A CIP catalogue record for this book is available from the British Library.

ISBN 978 1 78739 541 1

Editorial Director: Roland Hall
Design: Russell Knowles
Picture Research: Steve Behan
Production: Rachel Burgess

Printed in China

10 9 8 7 6 5 4 3 2 1

THE BEATLES

ILLUSTRATED LYRICS

WELBECK

CONTENTS

INTRODUCTION

BY STEVE TURNER

Paul once told me that he and John began writing songs because it was the only way that the Beatles could stay ahead of the local competition. They were tired of turning up to perform at clubs only to find that all the rare B-sides and LP tracks they'd learned from American imports had already been played by groups lower down on the bill. Hence was born the greatest songwriting partnership in rock 'n' roll history.

They discovered how to build by breaking down the rock classics and finding out how their various parts fitted together. Then they tested their versions on audiences who stood so close to them that they could tell by their eyes whether a number worked. They found that songs packed with personal pronouns were highly effective – 'I Saw Her Standing There', 'From Me To You', 'She Loves You'.

For the first two years of their recording career no one discussed their lyrics, except to decry their use of informalities such as "Yeah, yeah, yeah" (even Paul's dad thought it should be 'Yes, yes, yes"). In press conferences they were asked why they liked jelly babies but not how they wrote songs.

Then things changed. They began writing frankly about their lives rather than recycling clichés about diamond rings. Broadcaster Kenneth Allsop challenged John to put as much of himself into his songs as he did into *In His Own Write*, his book of stories, sketches and poems. Then Peter Sellers mockingly recorded *A Hard Day's Night* in the style of a Shakespearian monologue, exposing the lyric's easy rhymes and shallow story.

Paul's song 'She's A Woman' may have had the worst Beatle rhyme (presents/peasant) but it also had the first sly drug reference ("Turns me on when I get lonely"). On *Beatles For Sale* (1964) John's 'I'm A Loser' and 'I Don't Want To Spoil The Party' were candid admissions of inadequacy, not the normal fare of hit-making pop.

John always wrote like a wounded lover expecting the worst, whereas Paul wrote with the cocky optimism of a born winner. 'We Can Work It Out' was Paul at his positive best. John naturally wrote autobiographically while Paul created fiction populated with folk like Maxwell, Desmond, Eleanor, Vera, Chuck and Dave.

John's 'Nowhere Man' (1965) was the first album track not to be about love and Paul's 'Paperback Writer' (1966) the first single.

They were now not only growing up but coming under the influence of the burgeoning underground arts scenes in London and New York. They went from wanting to write songs like Chuck Berry to wanting to write songs like Andy Warhol or William Burroughs.

They flourished as lyricists in this environment and George gained in confidence. 'Eleanor Rigby' (Paul) was a beautifully told short story; 'Taxman' (George) was a piece of pop art (and the first Beatles' song to name real people); 'Yellow Submarine' (Paul) was a classic children's novelty song. Freed from the love song factory they now responded to different stimulae. 'Tomorrow Never Knows' was inspired by a book, 'Strawberry Fields Forever' by a Liverpool orphanage, and 'She's Leaving Home' by a newspaper story.

By the time they wrote *The Beatles* (the White Album) their different lyrical approaches had solidified. Paul was buoyant ('Martha My Dear', 'Birthday') and drawn to tale-telling ('Rocky Raccoon', 'Honey Pie'). John was languid ('I'm So Tired', 'Yer Blues') and paring his language back from the flowery excesses of psychedelia ('Happiness Is A Warm Gun'). They also became competitive, with Paul showing John how he could be tough minimalist ('Why Don't We Do It In The Road') and John showing Paul his sentimental side ('Julia', 'Good Night').

On *Let It Be* and *Abbey Road* they travelled further in these directions, John writing some of his most abstract and imaginative lyrics ('Across The Universe', 'Come Together') and Paul writing some of his most crowd-pleasing anthems ('The Long And Winding Road', 'Let It Be').

Are the words of the Beatles' songs poems? Not really. Poems have their own inbuilt music; lyrics are full of empty spaces awaiting the sounds of guitars, keyboards and drums to fill them out. But many of them used poetic techniques and many inspired poets. Significantly, they fulfilled the traditional function of poetry in uniting the tribe and articulating its hopes, fears and joys. Most of us can't recite a poem of Ted Hughes or Robert Frost from memory and yet we can sing along to 'All You Need Is Love' or 'Hey Jude'. Their words are lodged in our brains. And now 178 of the songs are in this handsome book, in chronological order of release. Enjoy.

Steve Turner, London, July 2020.

1, 2, 3, 4!

Well, she was just 17
You know what I mean
And the way she looked was way beyond compare
So how could I dance with another (Ooh)
When I saw her standing there

Well she looked at me, and I, I could see
That before too long I'd fall in love with her
She wouldn't dance with another (Whoo)
When I saw her standing there

Well, my heart went "boom"
When I crossed that room
And I held her hand in mine
Whoah, we danced through the night
And we held each other tight
And before too long I fell in love with her
Now I'll never dance with another (Whoo)
When I saw her standing there

Well, my heart went "boom"
When I crossed that room
And I held her hand in mine
Well, we danced through the night
And we held each other tight
And before too long I fell in love with her
Now I'll never dance with another (Whoo)
Since I saw her standing there

Since I saw her standing there
Since I saw her standing there

I SAW HER NDING THERE

MISERY

1 9 6 3

The world is treating me bad, misery

I'm the kind of guy
Who never used to cry
The world is treating me bad, misery

I've lost her now for sure
I won't see her no more
It's gonna be a drag, misery

I'll remember all the little things we've done
Can't she see she'll always be the only one, only one

Send her back to me
Cause everyone can see
Without her I will be in misery

I'll remember all the little things we've done
She'll remember and she'll miss her only one, lonely one

Send her back to me
Cause everyone can see
Without her I will be in misery (Oh oh oh)
In misery
(Ooh ee ooh ooh)
My misery
(La la la la la la)

AFTER HEARING
JOE BROWN's

HIT RECORD
"Picture of you"

see him in person
with his 'BRUVVERS

AT THE
TOWER BALLROOM
* NEW BRIGHTON

SUPPORTED BY THE NORTH'S GREATEST SOUND

the sensational 'BEATLES'

PLUS

THE NORTH'S FABULOUS Statesmen

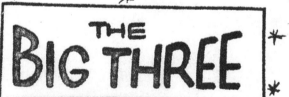

THE Big THREE

Steve Day AND THE DRIFTERS

the 4 JAYS

27 JULY 1962

Watch local press for details!

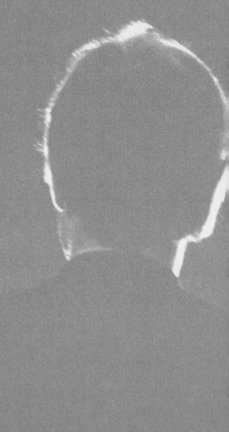

1963

You'll never know how much I really love you
You'll never know how much I really care

Listen
Do you want to know a secret
Do you promise not to tell, whoa oh, oh

Closer
Let me whisper in your ear
Say the words you long to hear
I'm in love with you

Listen
Do you want to know a secret
Do you promise not to tell, whoa oh, oh

Closer
Let me whisper in your ear
Say the words you long to hear
I'm in love with you

I've known the secret for a week or two
Nobody knows, just we two

Listen
Do you want to know a secret
Do you promise not to tell, whoa oh, oh

Closer
Let me whisper in your ear
Say the words you long to hear

I'm in love with you

"THE BEATLES COME TO TOWN"

PAUL

1963

THERE'S A PLACE

JOHN

There is a place
Where I can go
When I feel low
When I feel blue
And it's my mind
And there's no time when I'm alone

I think of you
And things you do
Go 'round my head
The things you said
Like "I love only you"

In my mind there's no sorrow
Don't you know that it's so
There'll be no sad tomorrow
Don't you know that it's so

TECHNICOLOR

There is a place
Where I can go
When I feel low
When I feel blue
And it's my mind
And there's no time when I'm alone

There's a place
There's a place
There's a place
There's a place

RINGO

GEORGE

Thank You Girl

1963

Oh, oh, you've been good to me
You made me glad
When I was blue
And eternally I'll always be
In love with you
And all I gotta do
Is thank you girl, thank you girl

I could tell the world
A thing or two about our love
I know little girl
Only a fool would doubt our love
And all I gotta do
Is thank you girl, thank you girl

Thank you girl for loving me
The way that you do (way that you do)
That's the kind of love
That is too good to be true
And all I gotta do
Is thank you girl, thank you girl

Oh, oh, you've been good to me
You made me glad
When I was blue
And eternally I'll always be
In love with you
And all I gotta do
Is thank you girl, thank you girl

Oh, oh, oh
Oh, oh, oh
Oh, oh

George Harrison   Ringo Starr   Paul McCartney   John Lennon

FROM ME TO YOU

1963

Da da da da da dum dum da
Da da da da da dum dum da

If there's anything that you want
If there's anything I can do
Just call on me and I'll send it along
With love, from me to you

I got everything that you want
Like a heart that's oh so true
Just call on me and I'll send it along
With love, from me to you

I got arms that long to hold you
And keep you by my side
I got lips that long to kiss you
And keep you satisfied, oooh

If there's anything that you want
If there's anything I can do
Just call on me and I'll send it along
With love, from me to you

From me, to you
Just call on me and I'll send it along
With love from me to you

I got arms that long to hold you
And keep you by my side
I got lips that long to kiss you
And keep you satisfied, oooh

If there's anything that you want
If there's anything I can do
Just call on me and I'll send it along
With love, from me to you
To you, to you, to you

SHE LOVES YOU

1963

She loves you, yeah, yeah,yeah
She loves you, yeah, yeah, yeah
She loves you, yeah, yeah, yeah, yeah

You think you've lost your love
Well, I saw her yesterday
It's you she's thinking of
And she told me what to say
She says she loves you
And you know that can't be bad
Yes, she loves you
And you know you should be glad

She said you hurt her so
She almost lost her mind
But now she says she knows
You're not the hurting kind
She says she loves you
And you know that can't be bad
Yes, she loves you
And you know you should be glad, ooh

She loves you, yeah, yeah, yeah
She loves you, yeah, yeah, yeah
And with a love like that
You know you should be glad

You know it's up to you
I think it's only fair
Pride can hurt you too
Apologise to her
Because she loves you
And you know that can't be bad
Yes, she loves you
And you know you should be glad, ooh

She loves you, yeah, yeah, yeah
She loves you, yeah, yeah, yeah
With a love like that
You know you should be glad
With a love like that
You know you should be glad
With a love like that
You know you should be glad
Yeah, yeah, yeah
Yeah, yeah, yeah, yeah

I'LL GET YOU 1963

Oh yeah, oh yeah
Oh yeah, oh yeah

Imagine I'm in love with you
It's easy cause I know
I've imagined I'm in love with you
Many, many, many times before

It's not like me to pretend
But I'll get you, I'll get you in the end
Yes I will, I'll get you in the end
Oh yeah, oh yeah

I think about you night and day
I need you and it's true
When I think about you, I can say
I'm never, never, never, never blue

So I'm telling you, my friend
That I'll get you, I'll get you in the end

Yes I will, I'll get you in the end
Oh yeah, oh yeah

Well, there's gonna be a time
When I'm gonna change your mind
So you might as well resign yourself to me
Oh yeah

Imagine I'm in love with you
It's easy cause I know
I've imagined I'm in love with you
Many, many, many times before

It's not like me to pretend
But I'll get you, I'll get you in the end
Yes I will, I'll get you in the end
Oh yeah, oh yeah
Oh yeah, oh yeah
Whoa yeah

IT WON'T BE LONG

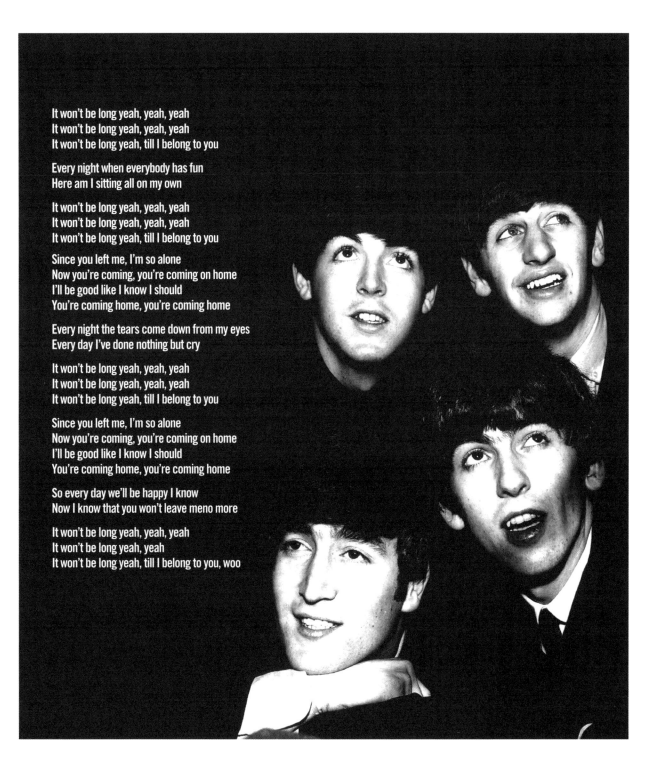

It won't be long yeah, yeah, yeah
It won't be long yeah, yeah, yeah
It won't be long yeah, till I belong to you

Every night when everybody has fun
Here am I sitting all on my own

It won't be long yeah, yeah, yeah
It won't be long yeah, yeah, yeah
It won't be long yeah, till I belong to you

Since you left me, I'm so alone
Now you're coming, you're coming on home
I'll be good like I know I should
You're coming home, you're coming home

Every night the tears come down from my eyes
Every day I've done nothing but cry

It won't be long yeah, yeah, yeah
It won't be long yeah, yeah, yeah
It won't be long yeah, till I belong to you

Since you left me, I'm so alone
Now you're coming, you're coming on home
I'll be good like I know I should
You're coming home, you're coming home

So every day we'll be happy I know
Now I know that you won't leave meno more

It won't be long yeah, yeah, yeah
It won't be long yeah, yeah
It won't be long yeah, till I belong to you, woo

Whenever I want you around, yeah
All I gotta do is call you on the phone
And you'll come running home
Yeah, that's all I gotta do

And when I, I wanna kiss you, yeah
All I gotta do is whisper in your ear
The words you long to hear
And I'll be kissing you

And the same goes for me
Whenever you want me at all
I'll be here yes I will
Whenever you call
You just gotta call on me, yeah
You just gotta call on me

And when I, I wanna kiss you, yeah
All I got to do is call you on the phone
And you'll come running how
Yeah, that's all I gotta do

And the same goes for me
Whenever you want me at all
I'll be here, yes I will
Whenever you call
You just gotta call on me
You just gotta call on me
Oh, you just gotta call on me

LITTLE CHILD

1963

Little child, little child
Little child, won't you dance with me?
I'm so sad and lonely
Baby, take a chance with me

Little child, little child
Little child, won't you dance with me?
I'm so sad and lonely
Baby, take a chance with me

If you want someone
To make you feel so fine
Then we'll have some fun
When you're mine, all mine
So come, come on, come on

Little child, little child
Little child, won't you dance with me?
I'm so sad and lonely
Baby, take a chance with me

When you're by my side
You're the only one
Don't you run and hide
Just come on, come on
So come on, come on, come on

Little child, little child,
Little child, won't you dance with me?
I'm so sad and lonely,
Baby, take a chance with me
Baby, take a chance with me
Baby, take a chance with me

Close your eyes and I'll kiss you
Tomorrow I'll miss you
Remember I'll always be true
And then while I'm away
I'll write home every day
And I'll send all my loving to you

I'll pretend that I'm kissing
The lips I am missing
And hope that my dreams will come true
And then while I'm away
I'll write home every day
And I'll send all my loving to you

All my loving, I will send to you
All my loving, darling I'll be true

Close your eyes and I'll kiss you
Tomorrow I'll miss you
Remember I'll always be true
And then while I'm away
I'll write home every day
And I'll send all my loving to you

All my loving, I will send to you
All my loving, darling I'll be true
All my loving, all my loving
Woo, all my loving, I will send to you

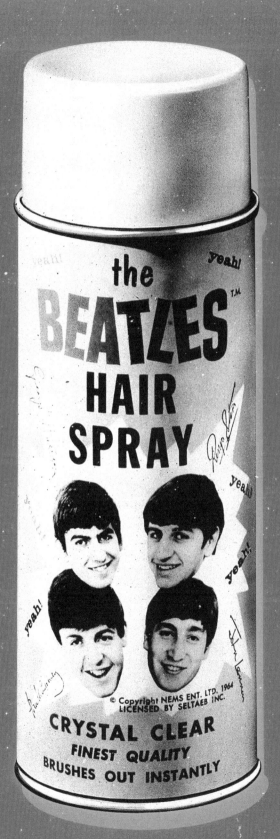

HOLD ME TIGHT 1963

It feels so right now, hold me tight
Tell me I'm the only one
And then I might
Never be the lonely one
So hold me tight, to-night, to-night
It's you, you you you

Hold me tight
Let me go on loving you
To-night to-night
Making love to only you
So hold me tight, to-night, to-night
It's you, you you you

Don't know what it means to hold you tight
Being here alone tonight with you
It feels so right now

Hold me tight
Tell me I'm the only one
And then I might
Never be the lonely one
So hold me tight, to-night, to-night
It's you, you you you

Don't know what it means to hold you tight
Being here alone tonight with you
It feels so right now

Hold me tight
Let me go on loving you
To-night, to-night
Making love to only you
So hold me tight, to-night, to-night
It's you, you you you oh, oh, oh, oh,
You oh oh

NOT A SECOND TIME 1963

You know you made me cry
I see no use in wondering why
I cry for you

And now you've changed your mind
I see no reason to change mine
I cry it's through, oh

You're giving me the same old line
I'm wondering why
You hurt me then
You're back again
No, no, no, not a second time

You know you made me cry
I see no use in wondering why
I cry for you, yeah

And now you've changed your mind
I see no reason to change mine
I cry it's through, oh

You're giving me the same old line
I'm wondering why
You hurt me then
You're back again
No, no, no, not a second time
Not a second time
Not the second time
No, no, no, no, no
No, no no

I WANNA BE YOUR MAN

1963

I wanna be your lover baby
I wanna be your man
I wanna be your lover baby
I wanna be your man

Love you like no other baby
Like no other can
Love you like no other baby
Like no other can

I wanna be your man, I wanna be your man
I wanna be your man, I wanna be your man

Tell me that you love me baby
Let me understand
Tell me that you love me baby
I wanna be your man

I wanna be your lover baby
I wanna be your man
I wanna be your lover baby
I wanna be your man

I wanna be your man, I wanna be your man
I wanna be your man, I wanna be your man

I wanna be your lover baby
I wanna be your man
I wanna be your lover baby
I wanna be your man

Love you like no other baby
Like no other can
Love you like no other baby
Like no other can

I wanna be your man, I wanna be your man
I wanna be your man, I wanna be your man
I wanna be your man, I wanna be your man

THIS BOY

1963

That boy took my love away
He'll regret it someday
But this boy wants you back again

That boy isn't good for you
Though he may want you too
This boy wants you back again

Oh, and this boy would be happy
Just to love you, but oh my
That boy won't be happy
Till he's seen you cry

This boy wouldn't mind the pain
Would always feel the same
If this boy gets you back again

This boy, this boy, this boy

I CALL YOUR NAME

1 9 6 3

I call your name
But you're not there
Was I to blame
For being unfair?

Oh, I can't sleep at night
Since you've been gone
I never weep at night
I can't go on

Don't you know I can't take it?
I don't know who can
I'm not gonna make it
I'm not that kind of man

Oh, I can't sleep at night
But just the same
I never weep at night
I call your name

Don't you know I can't take it?
I don't know who can
I'm not gonna make it
I'm not that kind of man

Oh, I can't sleep at night
But just the same
I never weep at night
I call your name
I call your name
I call your name

It's been a hard day's night
And I've been working like a dog
It's been a hard day's night
I should be sleeping like a log
But when I get home to you
I find the things that you do
Will make me feel alright

You know I work all day
To get you money to buy you things
And it's worth it just to hear you say
You're going to give me everything
So why on earth should I moan
Cause when I get you alone
You know I feel OK

When I'm home
Everything seems to be right
When I'm home feeling you holding me tight, tight

It's been a hard day's night
And I've been working like a dog
It's been a hard day's night
I should be sleeping like a log
But when I get home to you
I find the things that you do
Will make me feel alright, oww

So why on earth should I moan
Cause when I get you alone
You know I feel OK

When I'm home
Everything seems to be right
When I'm home feeling you holding me tight, tight

It's been a hard day's night
And I've been working like a dog
It's been a hard day's night,
I should be sleeping like a log
But when I get home to you
I find the things that you do
Will make me feel alright
You know I feel alright
You know I feel alright

A HARD DAY'S NIGHT

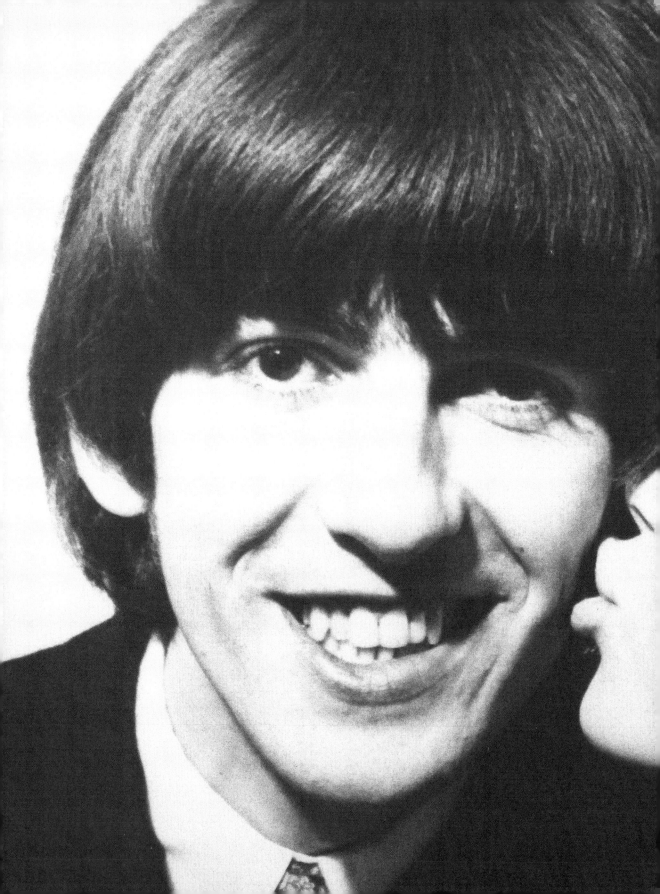

I SHOULD HAVE KNOWN BETTER 1964

I should have known better with a girl like you
That I would love everything that you do
And I do, hey, hey, hey, and I do

Whoa, oh, I never realised what a kiss could be
This could only happen to me
Can't you see, can't you see

That when I tell you that I love you, oh
You're gonna say you love me too, oh
And when I ask you to be mine
You're gonna say you love me too

So I should have realised a lot of things before
If this is love you've got to give me more
Give me more, hey hey hey, give me more

Whoa, oh, I never realised what a kiss could be
This could only happen to me
Can't you see, can't you see

That when I tell you that I love you, oh
You're gonna say you love me too, oh
And when I ask you to be mine
You're gonna say you love me too
You love me too, you love me too
You love me too

IF I F E L L

1964

If I fell in love with you
Would you promise to be true
And help me understand
Cause I've been in love before
And I found that love was more
Than just holding hands

If I give my heart to you
I must be sure
From the very start
That you would love me more than her

If I trust in you oh please
Don't run and hide
If I love you too oh please
Don't hurt my pride like her
Cause I couldn't stand the pain
And I would be sad if our new love
Was in vain

So I hope you see that I
Would love to love you
And that she will cry
When she learns we are two
Cause I couldn't stand the pain
And I would be sad if our new love
Was in vain

So I hope you see that I
Would love to love you
And that she will cry
When she learns we are two
If I fell in love with you

AND I LOVE HER

1964

I give her all my love
That's all I do
And if you saw my love
You'd love her too
I love her

She gives me everything
And tenderly
The kiss my lover brings
She brings to me
And I love her

A love like ours
Could never die
As long as I
Have you near me

Bright are the stars that shine
Dark is the sky
I know this love of mine
Will never die
And I love her

Bright are the stars that shine
Dark is the sky
I know this love of mine
Will never die
And I love her

I'M HAPPY JUST TO DANCE WITH YOU

1 9 6 4

Before this dance is through
I think I'll love you too
I'm so happy when you dance with me

I don't want to kiss or hold your hand
If it's funny try and understand
There is really nothing else I'd rather do
Cause I'm happy just to dance with you

I don't need to hug or hold you tight
I just want to dance with you all night
In this world there's nothing I would rather do
Cause I'm happy just to dance with you

Just to dance with you
Is everything I need
Before this dance is through
I think I'll love you too
I'm so happy when you dance with me

If somebody tries to take my place
Let's pretend we just can't see his face
In this world there's nothing I would rather do
Cause I'm happy just to dance with you

Just to dance with you
Is everything I need
Before this dance is through
I think I'll love you too
I'm so happy when you dance with me

If somebody tries to take my place
Let's pretend we just can't see his face
In this world there's nothing I would rather do
I've discovered I'm in love with you
Cause I'm happy just to dance with you

T E L L
M E
W H Y

Tell me why you cried
And why you lied to me
Tell me why you cried
And why you lied to me

Well I gave you everything I had
But you left me sitting on my own
Did you have to treat me oh so bad
All I do is hang my head and moan

Tell me why you cried
And why you lied to me
Tell me why you cried
And why you lied to me

If it's something that I've said or done
Tell me what and I'll apologise
If you don't I really can't go on
Holding back these tears in my eyes

Tell me why you cried
And why you lied to me
Tell me why you cried
And why you lied to me

Well, I'm beggin' on my bended knees
If you'll only listen to my pleas
Is there anything I can do
Cause I really can't stand it, I'm so in love with you

Tell me why you cried
And why you lied to me
Tell me why you cried
And why you lied to me

1964

CAN'T BUY ME LOVE 1964

Can't buy me love, love
Can't buy me love

I'll buy you a diamond ring my friend
  if it makes you feel alright
I'll get you anything my friend
  if it makes you feel alright
Cause I don't care too much for money
  money can't buy me love

I'll give you all I got to give
  if you say you'll love me too
I may not have a lot to give
  but what I got I'll give to you
I don't care too much for money
Money can't buy me love

Can't buy me love
Everybody tells me so
Can't buy me love
No no no, no

Say you don't need no diamond rings
  and I'll be satisfied
Tell me that you want the kind of things
  that money just can't buy
I don't care too much for money
Money can't buy me love
Owww

Can't buy me love
Everybody tells me so
Can't buy me love
No no no, no

Say you don't need no diamond rings
  and I'll be satisfied
Tell me that you want the kind of things
  that money just can't buy
I don't care too much for money
Money can't buy me love

Can't buy me love, love
Can't buy me love

HELP! BEATLES HELP!
© UNITED ARTISTS 1965

I'M 4 BEATLES

IN A YELLOW SUBMARINE

BEATLES HELP!
© UNITED ARTISTS 1965

BAND-AID. BRAND
plastic strip
John John PROD NEW DRU

I'M A BEATLE BUG

I'M A BEATLES BOOSTER

Geor Harri

Get Your BEATLES! TONS PE!

THE BEATLES
FAN CLUB

The BEATLES

The BEATLES

I·B·F·C MEMBERSHIP CARD

NO.

NAME

John Lennon

Ringo Starr

Paul McCartn

Geor

BEATLES' HAIR!

SUPPLY IS LIMITED
For that special Beatlemaniac.

ACTUALLY contains a lock of hair
from one of the Fab Fo

Yes BEATLE FANS...
Yesterday our trou-
bles seemed so far
away. So come to-
gether now and dis-
cover what millions
have before, that
LOVE is all you need!
Experience what
magic their mop-tops
brought to others.
Take this card, hold
tight and SHAKE!

SEALED WITH A KISS

FA

ANY TIME
AT ALL

1 9 6 4

Any time at all, any time at all
Any time at all, all you've gotta do is call
And I'll be there

If you need somebody to love
Just look into my eye
I'll be there to make you feel right

If you're feeling sorry and sad
I'd really sympathise
Don't you be sad, just call me tonight

Any time at all, any time at all
Any time at all, all you've gotta do is call
And I'll be there

If the sun has faded away
I'll try to make it shine
There is nothing I won't do
When you need a shoulder to cry
I hope it will be mine
Call me tonight, and I'll come to you

Any time at all, any time at all
Any time at all, all you've gotta do is call
And I'll be there
Any time at all, any time at all

Any time at all, all you've gotta do is call
And I'll be there
Any time at all, all you've gotta do is call
And I'll be there

I'LL CRY INSTEAD

I've got every reason on earth to be mad
Cause I've just lost the only girl I had
And if I could get my way
I'd get myself locked up today
But I can't so I'll cry instead

I've got a chip on my shoulder that's bigger than my feet
I can't talk to people that I meet
And if I could see you now
I'd try to make you sad somehow
But I can't so I'll cry instead

Don't want to cry when there's people there
I get shy when they start to stare
I'm gonna hide myself away, ay hay
But I'll come back again someday
And when I do you'd better hide all the girls
I'm gonna break their hearts all 'round the world
Yes, I'm gonna break them in two
And show you what your loving man can do
Until then I'll cry instead

Don't want to cry when there's people there
I get shy when they start to stare
I'm gonna hide myself away, ay hay
But I'll come back again someday
And when I do you'd better hide all the girls
Cause I'm gonna break their hearts all 'round the world
Yes, I'm gonna break them in two
And show you what your loving man can do
Until then I'll cry instead

WHEN I GET HOME

1964

Whoa-I, whoa-I
I got a whole lot of things to tell her
When I get home
Come on, out my way
Cause I'm gonna see my baby today
I've got a whole lot of things I've gotta say
To her

Whoa-I, whoa-I
I got a whole lot of things to tell her
When I get home
Come on if you please
I've got no time for trivialities
I've got a girl who's waiting home for me
Tonight

Whoa-I, whoa-I
I got a whole lot of things to tell her
When I get home
When I'm getting home tonight
I'm gonna hold her tight
I'm gonna love her till the cows come home
I bet I'll love her more
Till I walk out that door
Again

Come on, let me through
I've got so many things I've got to do
I've got no business being here with you
This way

Whoa-I, whoa-I
I've got a whole lot of things to tell her
When I get home, yeah
I've got a whole lot of things to tell her
When I get home

THINGS WE SAID TODAY
1964

You say you will love me
If I have to go
You'll be thinking of me
Somehow I will know
Someday when I'm lonely
Wishing you weren't so far away
Then I will remember
Things we said today

You say you'll be mine, girl
Till the end of time
These days such a kind girl
Seems so hard to find
Someday when we're dreaming
Deep in love, not a lot to say
Then we will remember
Things we said today

Me, I'm just the lucky guy
Love to hear you say that love is love
And though we may be blind
Love is here to stay and that's enough

To make you mine, girl
Be the only one
Love me all the time, girl
We'll go on and on
Someday when we're dreaming
Deep in love, not a lot to say
Then we will remember
Things we said today

Me, I'm just the lucky guy
Love to hear you say that love is love
Though we may be blind
Love is here to stay and that's enough

To make you mine, girl
Be the only one
Love me all the time, girl
We'll go on and on
Someday when we're dreaming
Deep in love, not a lot to say
Then we will remember
Things we said today

YOU CAN'T DO THAT

1964

I got something to say that might cause you pain
If I catch you talking to that boy again
I'm gonna let you down
And leave you flat
Because I told you before, oh
You can't do that

Well, it's the second time I've caught you talking to him
Do I have to tell you one more time, I think it's a sin
I think I'll let you down (Let you down)
Leave you flat (Gonna let you down and leave you flat)
Because I've told you before, oh
You can't do that

Everybody's green
Cause I'm the one who won your love
But if they'd seen
You talking that way they'd laugh in my face

So please listen to me, if you wanna stay mine
I can't help my feelings, I'd go out of my mind
I'm gonna let you down (Let you down)
And leave you flat (Gonna let you down and leave you flat)
Because I've told you before
Oh, you can't do that
You can't do that
You can't do that
You can't do that
You can't do that
You can't do that

I'LL BE BACK

1964

You know if you break my heart I'll go
But I'll be back again
Cause I told you once before goodbye
But I came back again

I love you so
I'm the one who wants you
Yes, I'm the one who wants you, oh ho, oh ho, oh

You could find better things to do
Than to break my heart again
This time I will try to show that I'm
Not trying to pretend

I thought that you would realise
That if I ran away from you
That you would want me too
But I got a big surprise
Oh ho, oh ho, oh

You could find better things to do
Than to break my heart again
This time I will try to show that I'm
Not trying to pretend

I wanna go but I hate to leave you
You know I hate to leave you, oh ho, oh ho, oh
You, if you break my heart I'll go
But I'll be back again

I FEEL

Baby's good to me you know
She's happy as can be you know
She said so
I'm in love with her and I feel fine

Baby says she's mine you know
She tells me all the time you know
She said so
I'm in love with her and I feel fine

I'm so glad that she's my little girl
She's so glad, she's telling all the world

That her baby buys her things you know
He buys her diamond rings you know
She said so
She's in love with me and I feel fine

Baby says she's mine you know
She tells me all the time you know
She said so
I'm in love with her and I feel fine

1964

I'm so glad that she's my little girl
She's so glad, she's telling all the world

That her baby buys her things you know
He buys her diamond rings you know
She said so
She's in love with me and I feel fine
She's in love with me and I feel fine

EIGHT DAYS A WEEK

Ooh I need your love babe
Guess you know it's true
Hope you need my love babe
Just like I need you
Hold me, love me, hold me, love me
I ain't got nothin' but love babe
Eight days a week

Love you every day girl
Always on my mind
One thing I can say girl
Love you all the time
Hold me, love me, hold me, love me
I ain't got nothing but love girl
Eight days a week

I love you
Eight days a week
Is not enough to show I care

Ooh I need your love babe
Guess you know it's true
Hope you need my love babe
Just like I need you
Hold me, love me, hold me, love me
Ain't got nothin' but love babe
Eight days a week

Eight days a week
I love you
Eight days a week
Is not enough to show I care

Love you every day girl
Always on my mind
One thing I can say girl
Love you all the time
Hold me, love me, hold me, love me I ain't
got nothin' but love babe
Eight days a week
Eight days a week
Eight days a week

1964

SHE'S A WOMAN

1964

My love don't give me presents
I know that she's no peasant
Only ever has to give me
Love forever and forever
My love don't give me presents
Turns me on when I get lonely
People tell me that she's only
Fooling, I know she isn't

She don't give boys the eye
She hates to see me cry
She is happy just to hear me
Say that I will never leave her
She don't give boys the eye

She will never make me jealous
Gives me all her time as well as loving
Don't ask me why

She's a woman who understands
She's a woman who loves her man

My love don't give me presents
I know that she's no peasant
Only ever has to give me
Love forever and forever
My love don't give me presents
Turns me on when I get lonely
People tell me that she's only
Fooling, I know she isn't, woo

She's a woman who understands
She's a woman who loves her man

My love don't give me presents
I know that she's no peasant
Only ever has to give me
Love forever and forever
My love don't give me presents
Turns me on when I get lonely
People tell me that she's only
Fooling, I know she isn't

She's a woman
She's a woman
She's a woman

I'M A LOSER 1964

I'm a loser
I'm a loser
And I'm not what I appear to be

Of all the love I have won or have lost
There is one love I should never have crossed
She was a girl in a million, my friend
I should have known she would win in the end

I'm a loser
And I lost someone who's near to me
I'm a loser
And I'm not what I appear to be

Although I laugh and I act like a clown
Beneath this mask I am wearing a frown
My tears are falling like rain from the sky
Is it for her or myself that I cry

I'm a loser
And I lost someone who's near to me
I'm a loser
And I'm not what I appear to be

What have I done to deserve such a fate
I realize I have left it too late
And so it's true, pride comes before a fall
I'm telling you so that you won't lose all

I'm a loser
And I lost someone who's near to me
I'm a loser
And I'm not what I appear to be

NO REPLY
1964

This happened once before
When I came to your door
No reply
They said it wasn't you
But I saw you peep through
Your window

I saw the light, I saw the light
I know that you saw me
Cause I looked up to see your face

I tried to telephone
They said you were not home
That's a lie
Cause I know where you've been
I saw you walk in your door

I nearly died, I nearly died
Cause you walked hand in hand
With another man in my place

If I were you I'd realise that I
Love you more than any other guy
And I'll forgive the lies that I
Heard before when you gave me
No reply

I've tried to telephone
They said you were not home
That's a lie
Cause I know where you've been
I saw you walk in your door

I nearly died, I nearly died
Cause you walked hand in hand
With another man in my place
No reply, no reply

I DON'T WANT TO SPOIL THE PARTY

1 9 6 4

I don't want to spoil the party so I'll go
I would hate my disappointment to show
There's nothing for me here so I will disappear
If she turns up while I'm gone please let me know

I've had a drink or two and I don't care
There's no fun in what I do if she's not there
I wonder what went wrong
I've waited far too long
I think I'll take a walk and look for her

Though tonight she's made me sad
I still love her
If I find her I'll be glad
I still love her

I don't want to spoil the party so I'll go
I would hate my disappointment to show
There's nothing for me here so I will disappear
If she turns up while I'm gone please let me know

Though tonight she's made me sad
I still love her
If I find her I'll be glad
I still love her

Though I've had a drink or two and I don't care
There's no fun in what I do if she's not there
I wonder what went wrong
I've waited far too long
I think I'll take a walk and look for her

I'LL FOLLOW THE SUN

One day you'll look to see I've gone
For tomorrow may rain, so I'll follow the sun
Some day you'll know I was the one
But tomorrow may rain, so I'll follow the sun

And now the time has come
And so my love I must go
And though I lose a friend
In the end you will know, oooh

One day you'll find that I have gone
But tomorrow may rain, so I'll follow the sun
Yea, tomorrow may rain, so I'll follow the sun

And now the time has come
And so my love I must go
And though I lose a friend
In the end you will know, oooh

One day you'll find that I have gone
But tomorrow may rain, so I'll follow the sun

1964

BABY'S IN BLACK

1 9 6 4

Oh dear, what can I do?
Baby's in black and I'm feeling blue
Tell me, oh what can I do?

She thinks of him
And so she dresses in black
And though he'll never come back
She's dressed in black
Oh dear, what can I do?
Baby's in black and I'm feeling blue
Tell me, oh what can I do?

I think of her
But she thinks only of him
And though it's only a whim
She thinks of him
Oh how long will it take
Till she sees the mistake she has made?
Dear what can I do?
Baby's in black and I'm feeling blue
Tell me, oh what can I do?

Oh how long will it take
Till she sees the mistake she has made?
Dear what can I do?
Baby's in black and I'm feeling blue
Tell me, oh what can I do?

She thinks of him and so
She dresses in black
And though he'll never come back
She's dressed in black
Oh dear, what can I do?
Baby's in black and I'm feeling blue
Tell me, oh what can I do?

EVERY
LITTLE THING 1964

When I'm walking beside her
People tell me I'm lucky
Yes, I know I'm a lucky guy
I remember the first time
I was lonely without her
Can't stop thinking about her now

Every little thing she does
She does for me, yeah
And you know the things she does
She does for me, oooh

When I'm with her I'm happy
Just to know that she loves me
Yes, I know that she loves me now
There is one thing I'm sure of
I will love her forever
For I know love will never die

Every little thing she does
She does for me, yeah
And you know the things she does
She does for me, oooh

Every little thing she does
She does for me, yeah
And you know the things she does
She does for me, oooh
Every little thing
Every little thing

WHAT YOU'RE DOING

1964

Look what you're doing
I'm feeling blue and lonely
Would it be too much to ask of you
What you're doing to me?

You got me running
And there's no fun in it
Why should it be so much to ask of you
What you're doing to me?

I've been waiting here for you
Wond'ring what you're gonna do
Should you need a love that's true
It's me

Please stop your lying
You've got me crying, girl
Why should it be so much to ask of you
What you're doing to me?

I've been waiting here for you
Wond'ring what you're gonna do
Should you need a love that's true
It's me

Please stop your lying
You've got me crying, girl
Why should it be so much to ask of you
What you're doing to me?
What you're doing to me?
What you're doing to me?

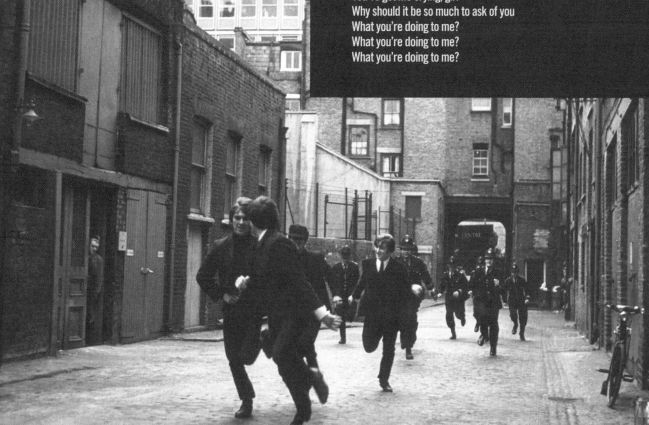

Yes it is

1965

If you wear red tonight
Remember what I said tonight
For red is the colour that my baby wore
And what's more, it's true
Yes it is

Scarlet were the clothes she wore
Everybody knows I'm sure
I would remember all the things we planned
Understand it's true
Yes it is, it's true
Yes it is

I could be happy with you by my side
If I could forget her, but it's my pride
Yes it is, yes it is, oh, yes it is, yeah

Please don't wear red tonight
This is what I said tonight
For red is the colour that will make me blue
In spite of you, it's true
Yes it is, it's true
Yes it is

I could be happy with you by my side
If I could forget her, but it's my pride
Yes it is, yes it is, oh, yes it is, yeah

Please don't wear red tonight
This is what I said tonight
For red is the colour that will make me blue
In spite of you, it's true
Yes it is, it's true
Yes it is, it's true

You tell lies thinking I can't see
You can't cry cause you're laughing at me
I'm down (I'm really down)
I'm down (Down on the ground)
I'm down (I'm really down)

How can you laugh
When you know I'm down?
How can you laugh
When you know I'm down?

Man buys ring, woman throws it away
Same old thing happen every day
I'm down (I'm really down)
I'm down (Down on the ground)
I'm down (I'm really down)

How can you laugh
When you know I'm down?
How can you laugh
When you know I'm down?

We're all alone and there's nobody else
You'll still moan, "Keep your hands to yourself"
I'm down (I'm really down)
Ah babe I'm down (Down on the ground)
I'm down (I'm really down)

How can you laugh
When you know I'm down?
How can you laugh
When you know I'm down? Whoa-ow

Ah babe you know I'm down (I'm really down)
I guess I'm down (I'm really down)
I'm down on the ground (I'm really down)
I'm down (I'm really down)
Ah, baby I'm upside down
Oh yeah, yeah, yeah, yeah, yeah, yeah

(I'm really down)
Oh baby I'm down (I'm really down)
I'm feeling upside down (I'm really down)
Ohh, I'm down (I'm really down)
Oh baby I'm down, yeah
Oh baby I'm down, yeah

Oh baby I'm down (I'm really down)
Oh baby I'm down (I'm really down)
Oh baby, baby, baby (I'm really down)
Oh baby I'm down (I'm really down)

I'M DOWN
1 9 6 5

STOP WORRYING!

IS ON THE WAY!

The Colorful Adventures of

THE BEATLES

are more Colorful than ever...in COLOR!

HELP YOURSELF TO SEVEN GREAT NEW BEATLE HITS!

ALSO STARRING
LEO McKERN   ELEANOR BRON   VICTOR SPINETTI   ROY KINNEAR   PRODUCED BY WALTER SHENSON

SCREENPLAY BY   STORY BY   DIRECTED BY   A WALTER SHENSON–
MARC BEHM and CHARLES WOOD   MARC BEHM   RICHARD LESTER   EASTMANCOLOR   SUBAFILMS   A UNITED ARTISTS RELEASE
                                                                                           PRODUCTION

HELP!

Help! I need somebody
Help! Not just anybody
Help! You know I need someone
Help!

When I was younger so much younger than today
I never needed anybody's help in any way
But now these days are gone, I'm not so self assured
Now I find I've changed my mind I've opened up the doors

Help me if you can, I'm feeling down
And I do appreciate you being 'round
Help me get my feet back on the ground
Won't you please, please help me

And now my life has changed in oh so many ways
My independence seems to vanish in the haze
But every now and then I feel so insecure
I know that I just need you like I've never done before

Help me if you can, I'm feeling down
And I do appreciate you being 'round
Help me get my feet back on the ground
Won't you please, please help me

When I was younger so much younger than today
I never needed anybody's help in any way
But now these days are gone, I'm not so self assured
Now I find I've changed my mind I've opened up the doors

Help me if you can, I'm feeling down
And I do appreciate you being 'round
Help me get my feet back on the ground
Won't you please, please help me,
help me, help me, ooh

1965

THE NIGHT BEFORE
1965

We said our goodbyes, ah, the night before
Love was in your eyes, ah, the night before
Now today I find
You have changed your mind
Treat me like you did the night before

Were you telling lies, ah, the night before?
Was I so unwise, ah, the night before?
When I held you near
You were so sincere
Treat me like you did the night before

Last night is a night I will remember you by
When I think of things we did it makes me wanna cry

We said our goodbyes, ah, the night before
Love was in your eyes, ah, the night before
Now today I find
You have changed your mind
Treat me like you did the night before

YOU'VE
GOT TO

Here I stand head in hand
Turn my face to the wall
If she's gone I can't go on
Feeling two-foot small

Everywhere people stare
Each and every day
I can see them laugh at me
And I hear them say

Hey, you've got to hide your love away
Hey, you've got to hide your love away

How can I even try
I can never win
Hearing them, seeing them
In the state I'm in

How could she say to me
Love will find a way
Gather round all you clowns
Let me hear you say

Hey, you've got to hide your love away
Hey, you've got to hide your love away

HIDE YOUR
LOVE AWAY

1965

I NEED YOU 1965

You don't realise how much I need you
Love you all the time and never leave you
Please come on back to me
I'm lonely as can be
I need you

Said you had a thing or two to tell me
How was I to know you would upset me?
I didn't realise as I looked in your eyes
You told me, oh yes, you told me,
you don't want my lovin' anymore
That's when it hurt me and feeling like this
I just can't go on anymore

Please remember how I feel about you
I could never really live without you
So, come on back and see
Just what you mean to me
I need you

But when you told me you don't want my lovin' anymore
That's when it hurt me and feeling like this
I just can't go on anymore

Please remember how I feel about you
I could never really live without you
So, come on back and see
Just what you mean to me
I need you
I need you
I need you

ANOTHER GIRL
1965

For I have got another girl
Another girl
You're making me say that I've got nobody but you
But as from today, well I've got somebody that's new
I ain't no fool and I don't take what I don't want
For I have got
Another girl
Another girl

She's sweeter than all the girls and I met quite a few
Nobody in all the world can do what she can do
And so I'm telling you, "This time you'd better stop"
For I have got
Another girl
Another girl who will love me till the end
Through thick and thin she will always be my friend

I don't want to say that I've been unhappy with you
But, as from today, well I've seen somebody that's new
I ain't no fool and I don't take what I don't want
For I have got
Another girl,
Another girl who will love me till the end
Through thick and thin she will always be my friend

I don't want to say that I've been unhappy with you
But, as from today, well, I've seen somebody that's new
I ain't no fool and I don't take what I don't want
For I have got
Another girl
Another girl
Another girl

YOU'RE GOING TO LOSE THAT GIRL 1965

You're going to lose that girl
(Yes, yes, you're gonna lose that girl)
You're going to lose that girl
(Yes, yes, you're gonna lose that girl)

If you don't take her out tonight
She's going to change her mind
(She's gonna change her mind)
And I will take her out tonight
And I will treat her kind
(I'm gonna treat her kind)

You're going to lose that girl
(Yes, yes, you're gonna lose that girl)
You're going to lose that girl
(Yes, yes, you're gonna lose that girl)

If you don't treat her right, my friend
You're going to find her gone
(You're gonna find her gone)
Cause I will treat her right, and then
You'll be the lonely one
(You're not the only one)

You're going to lose that girl
(Yes, yes, you're gonna lose that girl)
You're going to lose that girl
(Yes, yes, you're gonna lose that girl)
You're going to lose that girl
(Yes, yes, you're gonna lose that girl)

I'll make a point of taking her away from you,
(watch what you do) yeah
The way you treat her what else can I do?

(You're gonna lose that girl)
(You're gonna lose that girl)

You're going to lose that girl
(Yes, yes, you're gonna lose that girl)

You're going to lose that girl
(Yes, yes, you're gonna lose that girl)
You're going to lose that girl
(Yes, yes, you're gonna lose that girl)

I'll make a point of taking her away from you,
(watch what you do) yeah
The way you treat her what else can I do?

If you don't take her out tonight
She's going to change her mind
(She's gonna change her mind)
And I will take her out tonight
And I will treat her kind
(I'm gonna treat her kind)

You're going to lose that girl
(Yes, yes, you're gonna lose that girl)
You're going to lose that girl
(Yes, yes, you're gonna lose that girl)
You're going to lose that girl
(Yes, yes, you're gonna lose that girl)

RAIN CHECK — SEE REVERSE SIDE

TICKET TO RIDE
1965

I think I'm gonna be sad
I think it's today, yeah
The girl that's driving me mad
Is going away, yeah

She's got a ticket to ride
She's got a ticket to ride
She's got a ticket to ride
But she don't care

She said that living with me
Is bringing her down, yeah
For she would never be free
When I was around

She's got a ticket to ride
She's got a ticket to ride
She's got a ticket to ride
But she don't care

I don't know why she's riding so high
She ought to think twice
She ought to do right by me
Before she gets to saying goodbye
She ought to think twice
She ought to do right by me

I think I'm gonna be sad
I think it's today, yeah
The girl that's driving me mad
Is going away, yeah

Oh, she's got a ticket to ride
She's got a ticket to ride
She's got a ticket to ride
But she don't care

I don't know why she's riding so high
She ought to think twice
She ought to do right by me
Before she gets to saying goodbye
She ought to think twice
She ought to do right by me

She said that living with me
Is bringing her down, yeah
For she would never be free
When I was around

Ah, she's got a ticket to ride
She's got a ticket to ride
She's got a ticket to ride
But she don't care

My baby don't care, my baby don't care
My baby don't care, my baby don't care
My baby don't care, my baby don't care

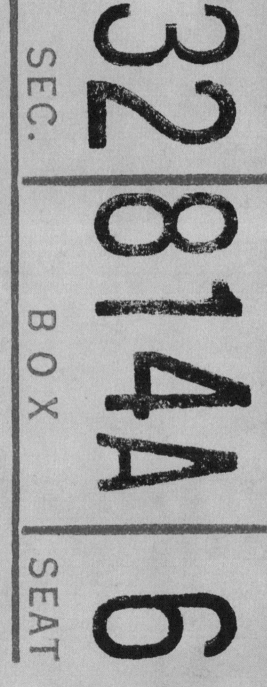

SHEA STADIUM

ENTER GATE

UPPER BOX $5.65

A

SEC. 32

BOX 814A

SEAT 6

SUN., AUG. 15, 1965-8 P.M.

TELL ME WHAT YOU SEE
1965

If you let me take your heart I will prove to you
We will never be apart if I'm part of you
Open up your eyes now, tell me what you see
It is no surprise now, what you see is me

Big and black the clouds may be, time will pass away
If you put your trust in me I'll make bright your day
Look into these eyes now, tell me what you see
Don't you realise now, what you see is me
Tell me what you see

Listen to me one more time, how can I get through?
Can't you try to see that I'm trying to get to you?
Open up your eyes now, tell me what you see
It is no surprise now, what you see is me
Tell me what you see

Listen to me one more time, how can I get through?
Can't you try to see that I'm trying to get to you?
Open up your eyes now, tell me what you see
It is no surprise now, what you see is me

Though you've gone away this morning
You'll be back again tonight
Telling me there'll be no next time
If I don't just don't treat you right
You'll never leave me and you know it's true
Cause you like me too much and I like you

You've tried before to leave me
But you haven't got the nerve
To walk out and make me lonely
Which is all that I deserve
You'll never leave me and you know it's true
Cause you like me too much and I like you

I really do
And it's nice when you believe me
If you leave me
I will follow you and bring you back where you belong
Cause I could't really stand it I'd admit that I was wrong
I wouldn't let you leave me cause it's true
Cause you like me too much and I like you

Cause you like me too much and I like you
I really do
And it's nice when you believe me
If you leave me
I will follow you and bring you back where you belong
Cause I could't really stand it I'd admit that I was wrong
I wouldn't let you leave me cause it's true
Cause you like me too much and I like you
Cause you like me too much and I like you

you like me too much 1965

POLICE LINE
POLICE

IT'S ONLY LOVE

1965

I get high when I see you go by
My oh my
When you sigh, my, my inside just flies
Butterflies
Why am I so shy when I'm beside you?

It's only love and that is all
Why should I feel the way I do?
It's only love, and that is all
But it's so hard loving you

Is it right that you and I should fight
Every night?
Just the sight of you makes nighttime bright
Very bright
Haven't I the right to make it up girl?

It's only love and that is all
Why should I feel the way I do?
It's only love, and that is all
But it's so hard loving you
Yes it's so hard loving you, loving you

I've just seen a face

1965

I've just seen a face
I can't forget the time or place
Where we just met
She's just the girl for me
And I want all the world to see
We've met, mmm-mmm-mmm-m'mmmmmm

Had it been another day
I might have looked the other way
And I'd have never been aware
But as it is I'll dream of her
Tonight, di-di-di-di'n'di
Falling, yes I am falling
And she keeps calling
Me back again

I have never known
The like of this, I've been alone
And I have missed things
And kept out of sight
But other girls were never quite
Like this, da-da-n'da-da'n'da
Falling, yes I am falling
And she keeps calling
Me back again

Falling, yes I am falling
And she keeps calling
Me back again

I've just seen a face
I can't forget the time or place
Where we just met
She's just the girl for me
And I want all the world to see
We've met,
mmm-mmm-mmm-da-da-da
Falling, yes I am falling
And she keeps calling
Me back again
Falling, yes I am falling
And she keeps calling
Me back again
Oh, falling, yes I am falling
And she keeps calling
Me back again

YESTERDAY

1965

Yesterday all my troubles seemed so far away
Now it looks as though they're here to stay
Oh, I believe in yesterday

Suddenly I'm not half the man I used to be
There's a shadow hanging over me
Oh, yesterday came suddenly

Why she had to go, I don't know, she wouldn't say
I said something wrong, now I long for yesterday

Yesterday love was such an easy game to play
Now I need a place to hide away
Oh, I believe in yesterday

Why she had to go, I don't know, she wouldn't say
I said something wrong, now I long for yesterday

Yesterday love was such an easy game to play
Now I need a place to hide away
Oh, I believe in yesterday

Mm mm mm mm mm mm mm

Got a good reason
For taking the easy way out
Got a good reason
For taking the easy way out now

She was a day tripper
One way ticket, yeah
It took me so long to find out
And I found out

She's a big teaser
She took me half the way there
She's a big teaser
She took me half the way there now

She was a day tripper
One way ticket, yeah
It took me so long to find out
And I found out
Ah,ah,ah,ah,ah,ah

DAY TR

Tried to please her
She only played one night stands
Tried to please her
She only played one night stands now

She was a day tripper
Sunday driver, yeah
It took me so long to find out
And I found out

Day tripper, day tripper, yeah
Day tripper, day tripper, yeah
Day tripper

WE CAN WORK IT OUT 1965

Try to see it my way
Do I have to keep on talking
Till I can't go on?

While you see it your way
Run the risk of knowing that
Our love may soon be gone
We can work it out
We can work it out

Think of what you're saying
You can get it wrong and still
You think that it's all right

Think of what I'm saying
We can work it out and
Get it straight or say good night
We can work it out
We can work it out

Life is very short
And there's no time
For fussing and fighting, my friend

I have always thought
That it's a crime
So I will ask you once again

Try to see it my way
Only time will tell
If I am right or I am wrong

While you see it your way
There's a chance that we might
Fall apart before too long
We can work it out
We can work it out

Life is very short
And there's no time
For fussing and fighting, my friend

I have always thought
That it's a crime
So I will ask you once again

Try to see it my way
Only time will tell
If I am right or I am wrong

While you see it your way
There's a chance that we might
Fall apart before too long
We can work it out
We can work it out

Asked a girl what she wanted to be
She said baby, "Can't you see
I wanna be famous, a star of the screen
But you can do something in between"

Baby you can drive my car
Yes I'm gonna be a star
Baby you can drive my car
And maybe I'll love you

I told a girl that my prospects were good
And she said "Baby, it's understood
Working for peanuts is all very fine
But I can show you a better time"

Baby you can drive my car
Yes I'm gonna be a star
Baby you can drive my car
And maybe I'll love you
Beep beep'n beep beep yeah

Baby you can drive my car
Yes I'm gonna be a star
Baby you can drive my car
And maybe I'll love you

I told that girl I can start right away
And she said, "Listen baby
I got something to say
I got no car and it's breaking my heart
But I've found a driver and that's a start"

Baby you can drive my car
Yes I'm gonna be a star
Baby you can drive my car
And maybe I'll love you
Beep beep'n beep beep yeah
Beep beep'n beep beep yeah
Beep beep'n beep beep yeah
Beep beep'n beep beep yeah

Drive my car

1965

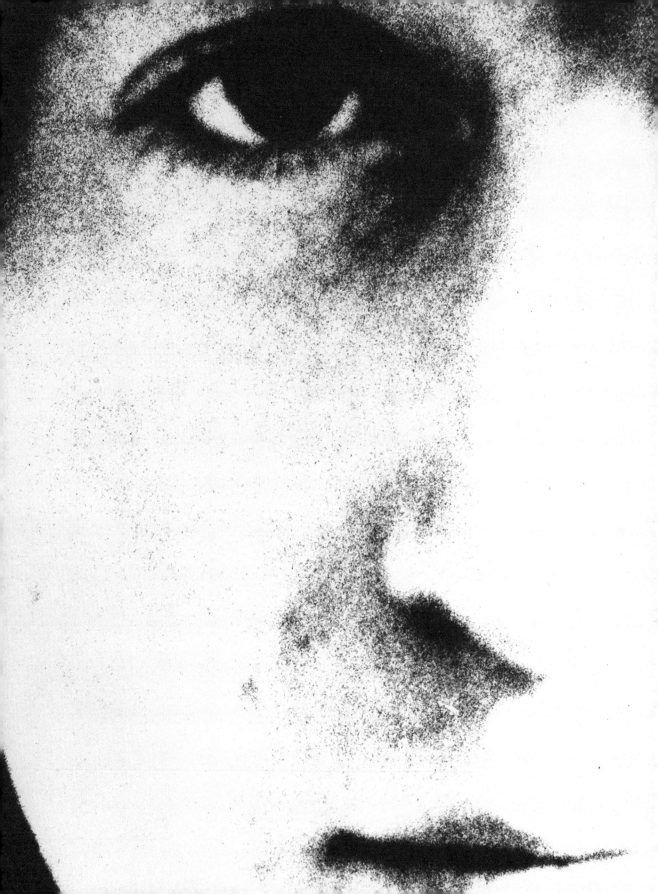

Norwegian Wood 1965

I once had a girl, or should I say, she once had me
She showed me her room, isn't it good, Norwegian wood?

She asked me to stay and she told me to sit anywhere
So I looked around and I noticed there wasn't a chair

I sat on the rug, biding my time, drinking her wine
We talked until two and then she said, "It's time for bed"

She told me she worked in the morning and started to laugh
I told her I didn't and crawled off to sleep in the bath

And when I awoke I was alone, this bird had flown
So I lit a fire, isn't it good, Norwegian wood?

YOU WON'T SEE ME

1965

When I call you up
Your line's engaged
I have had enough
So act your age
We have lost the time
That was so hard to find
And I will lose my mind
If you won't see me (You won't see me)
You won't see me (You won't see me)

I don't know why you
Should want to hide
But I can't get through
My hands are tied
I won't want to stay
I don't have much to say
But I can turn away
And you won't see me (You won't see me)
You won't see me (You won't see me)

Time after time
You refused to even listen
I wouldn't mind
If I knew what I was missing

Though the days are few
They're filled with tears
And since I lost you
It feels like years
Yes, it seems so long
Girl, since you've been gone
And I just can't go on
If you won't see me (You won't see me)
You won't see me (You won't see me)

Time after time
You refused to even listen
I wouldn't mind
If I knew (no I wouldn't)
What I was missing (no I wouldn't)

Though the days are few
They're filled with tears
And since I lost you
It feels like years
Yes, it seems so long
Girl, since you've been gone
And I just can't go on
If you won't see me (You won't see me)
You won't see me (You won't see me)

NOWHERE M
NOWHERE M
NOWHERE M
NOWHERE M
NOWHERE M
NOWHERE M
NOWHERE M
NOWHERE M
NOWHERE M

1965
NOWHERE MAN

He's a real Nowhere Man
Sitting in his nowhere land
Making all his nowhere plans for nobody

Doesn't have a point of view
Knows not where he's going to
Isn't he a bit like you and me?

Nowhere Man, please listen
You don't know what you're missing
Nowhere Man
The world's at your command

He's as blind as he can be
Just sees what he wants to see
Nowhere Man can you see me at all?

Nowhere Man, don't worry
Take your time, don't hurry
Leave it all till somebody else
Lends you a hand

Doesn't have a point of view
Knows not where he's going to
Isn't he a bit like you and me?

Nowhere Man, please listen
You don't know what you're missing
Nowhere Man
The world is at your command

He's a real Nowhere Man
Sitting in his nowhere land
Making all his nowhere plans for nobody
Making all his nowhere plans for nobody
Making all his nowhere plans for nobody

THINK FOR YOURSELF

1965

I've got a word or two
To say about the things that you do
You're telling all those lies
About the good things that we can have
If we close our eyes

Do what you want to do
And go where you're going to
Think for yourself
I won't be there with you

I left you far behind
The ruins of the life that you have in mind
And though you still can't see
I know your mind's made up
You're gonna cause more misery

Do what you want to do
And go where you're going to
Think for yourself
Cause I won't be there with you

Although your mind's opaque
Try thinking more if just for your own sake
The future still looks good
And you've got time to rectify
All the things that you should

Do what you want to do
And go where you're going to
Think for yourself
Cause I won't be there with you

Do what you want to do
And go where you're going to
Think for yourself
Cause I won't be there with you
Think for yourself
Cause I won't be there with you

THE WORD

1965

Say the word and you'll be free
Say the word and be like me
Say the word I'm thinking of
Have you heard the word is love?
It's so fine, it's sunshine
It's the word, love

In the beginning I misunderstood
But now I've got it, the word is good

Spread the word and you'll be free
Spread the word and be like me
Spread the word I'm thinking of
Have you heard the word is love?
It's so fine, it's sunshine
It's the word, love

Everywhere I go I hear it said
In the good and bad books that I have read

Say the word and you'll be free
Say the word and be like me
Say the word I'm thinking of
Have you heard the word is love?
It's so fine, it's sunshine
It's the word, love

Now that I know what I feel must be right
I'm here to show everybody the light

Give the word a chance to say
That the word is just the way
It's the word I'm thinking of
And the only word is love
It's so fine, it's sunshine
It's the word, love

Say the word, love
Say the word, love
Say the word, love
Say the word, love

Michelle, ma belle
These are words that go together well
My Michelle

Michelle, ma belle
Sont les mots qui vont tres bien ensemble
Tres bien ensemble

I love you, I love you, I love you
That's all I want to say
Until I find a way
I will say the only words I know
That you'll understand

Michelle, ma belle
Sont les mots qui vont tres bien ensemble
Tres bien ensemble

I need to, I need to, I need to
I need to make you see
Oh, what you mean to me
Until I do I'm hoping you will
Know what I mean

I love you

I want you, I want you, I want you
I think you know by now
I'll get to you somehow
Until I do I'm telling you
So you'll understand

Michelle, ma belle
Sont les mots qui vont tres bien ensemble
Tres bien ensemble

I will say the only words I know
That you'll understand, my Michelle

1965

What goes on in your heart?
What goes on in your mind?
You are tearing me apart
When you treat me so unkind
What goes on in your mind?

The other day I saw you
As I walked along the road
But when I saw him with you
I could feel my future fold
It's so easy for a girl like you to lie
Tell me why

What goes on in your heart?
What goes on in your mind?
You are tearing me apart
When you treat me so unkind
What goes on in your mind?

I met you in the morning
Waiting for the tides of time
But now the tide is turning
I can see that I was blind
It's so easy for a girl like you to lie
Tell me why

What goes on in your heart?

I used to think of no one else
But you were just the same
You didn't even think of me
As someone with a name
Did you mean to break my heart
and watch me die
Tell me why

What goes on in your heart?
What goes on in your mind?
You are tearing me apart
When you treat me so unkind
What goes on in your mind?

GIRL

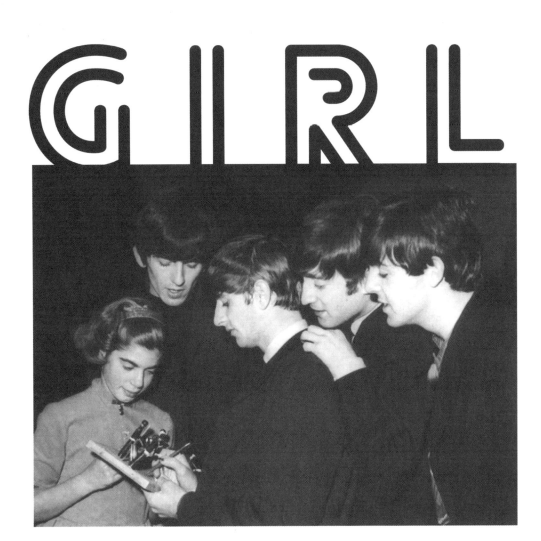

1965

Is there anybody going to listen to my story
All about the girl who came to stay?
She's the kind of girl you want so much it makes you sorry
Still, you don't regret a single day
Ah girl, girl

When I think of all the times I've tried so hard to leave her
She will turn to me and start to cry
And she promises the earth to me and I believe her
After all this time I don't know why
Ah girl, girl

She's the kind of girl who puts you down
When friends are there, you feel a fool
When you say she's looking good
She acts as if it's understood
She's cool, ooh, ooh, ooh
Girl, girl

Was she told when she was young
That pain would lead to pleasure?
Did she understand it when they said
That a man must break his back to earn his day of leisure?
Will she still believe it when he's dead?

Ah girl, girl, girl
Ah girl, girl, girl

I'M LOOKING
UOY HƎUOЯHT

1965

I'm looking through you
Where did you go?
I thought I knew you, what did I know?
You don't look different,
But you have changed
I'm looking through you
You're not the same

Your lips are moving, I cannot hear
Your voice is soothing
But the words aren't clear
You don't sound different
I've learned the game
I'm looking through you
You're not the same

Why, tell me why
Did you not treat me right?
Love has a nasty habit
Of disappearing overnight

You're thinking of me, the same old way
You were above me, but not today
The only difference is you're down there
I'm looking through you
And you're nowhere

Why, tell me why
Did you not treat me right?
Love has a nasty habit
Of disappearing overnight

I'm looking through you
Where did you go
I thought I knew you, what did I know
You don't look different
But you have changed
I'm looking through you
You're not the same

Yeah
Oh baby I'm changed

It's been a long time
Now I'm coming back home
I've been away now
Oh how, I've been alone

Wait till I come back to your side
We'll forget the tears we've cried

But if your heart breaks
Don't wait, turn me away
And if your heart's strong
Hold on, I won't delay

Wait till I come back to your side
We'll forget the tears we've cried

I feel as though
You ought to know
That I've been good
As good as I can be
And if you do
I'll trust in you
And know that you
Will wait for me

It's been a long time
Now I'm coming back home
I've been away now
Oh how, I've been alone

Wait till I come back to your side
We'll forget the tears we've cried

I feel as though
You ought to know
That I've been good
As good as I can be
And if you do
I'll trust in you
And know that you
Will wait for me

But if your heart breaks
Don't wait, turn me away
And if your heart's strong
Hold on, I won't delay

Wait till I come back to your side
We'll forget the tears we've cried

It's been a long time
Now I'm coming back home
I've been away now
Oh how, I've been alone

1965

LIFE

The Beatle Invasion

Fab Four in a
Miami Pool

IN MY LIFE

1 9 6 5

There are places I remember
All my life though some have changed
Some forever not for better
Some have gone and some remain
All these places have their moments
With lovers and friends I still can recall
Some are dead and some are living
In my life I've loved them all

But of all these friends and lovers
There is no one compares with you
And these memories lose their meaning
When I think of love as something new
Though I know I'll never lose affection
For people and things that went before
I know I'll often stop and think about them
In my life I love you more

Though I know I'll never lose affection
For people and things that went before
I know I'll often stop and think about them
In my life I love you more

In my life I love you more

If I needed someone to love
You're the one that I'd be thinking of
If I needed someone

If I had some more time to spend
Then I guess I'd be with you my friend
If I needed someone

Had you come some other day
Then it might not have been like this
But you see now I'm too much in love

Carve your number on my wall
And maybe you will get a call from me
If I needed someone
Ah, ah, ah, ah

If I had some more time to spend
Then I guess I'd be with you my friend
If I needed someone

Had you come some other day
Then it might not have been like this
But you see now I'm too much in love

Carve your number on my wall
And maybe you will get a call from me
If I needed someone
Ah, ah

IF I NEEDED SOMEONE

1966

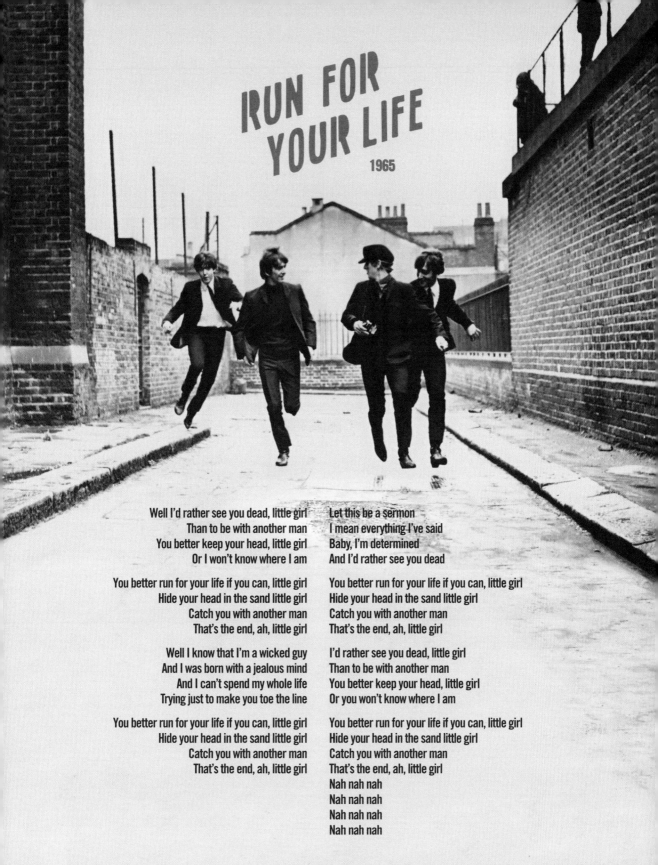

RUN FOR YOUR LIFE

1965

Well I'd rather see you dead, little girl
Than to be with another man
You better keep your head, little girl
Or I won't know where I am

You better run for your life if you can, little girl
Hide your head in the sand little girl
Catch you with another man
That's the end, ah, little girl

Well I know that I'm a wicked guy
And I was born with a jealous mind
And I can't spend my whole life
Trying just to make you toe the line

You better run for your life if you can, little girl
Hide your head in the sand little girl
Catch you with another man
That's the end, ah, little girl

Let this be a sermon
I mean everything I've said
Baby, I'm determined
And I'd rather see you dead

You better run for your life if you can, little girl
Hide your head in the sand little girl
Catch you with another man
That's the end, ah, little girl

I'd rather see you dead, little girl
Than to be with another man
You better keep your head, little girl
Or you won't know where I am

You better run for your life if you can, little girl
Hide your head in the sand little girl
Catch you with another man
That's the end, ah, little girl
Nah nah nah
Nah nah nah
Nah nah nah
Nah nah nah

Pape write

1966

Paperback writer, writer, writer
Dear Sir or Madam, will you read my book?
It took me years to write, will you take a look?
It's based on a novel by a man named Lear
And I need a job, so I want to be a paperback writer
Paperback writer

It's a dirty story of a dirty man
And his clinging wife doesn't understand
His son is working for the Daily Mail
It's a steady job but he wants to be a paperback writer
Paperback writer

Paperback writer

It's a thousand pages, give or take a few
I'll be writing more in a week or two
I can make it longer if you like the style
I can change it round and I want to be a paperback writer
Paperback writer

If you really like it you can have the rights
It could make a million for you overnight
If you must return it, you can send it here
But I need a break and I want to be a paperback writer
Paperback writer

Paperback writer
Paperback writer, paperback writer
Paperback writer, paperback writer
Paperback writer, paperback writer
Paperback writer, paperback writer

Raining 1966

If the rain comes they run and hide their heads
They might as well be dead
If the rain comes, if the rain comes

When the sun shines they slip into the shade
(When the sun shines down)
And drink their lemonade
(When the sun shines down)
When the sun shines
When the sun shines

Rain, I don't mind
Shine, the weather's fine

I can show you that when it starts to rain
(When the rain comes down)
Everything's the same
(When the rain comes down)
I can show you, I can show you

Rain, I don't mind
Shine, the weather's fine

Can you hear me, that when it rains and shines
(When it rains and shines)
It's just a state of mind?
(When it rains and shines)
Can you hear me, can you hear me?

Sdaeh rieht edih dna nur yeht semoc niar eht fI
(Rain)
niaR
(Rain)
niaR, enihsnuS

446, 101
176, 915
184, 840
112, 816
184, 489
211, 509

1, 317, 000

20,065
26,501
32,216
18,788
38,414

13,916
12,721
17,645
30,574
38,315

23,722
26,395
25,950
36,480
48,961
24,425
───────
459,218

TAXMAN
1966

1-2-3-4, 1-2-3-4
Let me tell you how it will be
There's one for you, nineteen for me

Cause I'm the taxman
Yeah, I'm the taxman

Should five per cent appear too small
Be thankful I don't take it all
Cause I'm the taxman, yeah I'm the taxman

If you drive a car, I'll tax the street
If you try to sit, I'll tax your seat
If you get too cold, I'll tax the heat
If you take a walk, I'll tax your feet

Taxman!
Cause I'm the taxman, yeah I'm the taxman

Don't ask me what I want it for
(Aha, Mr. Wilson)
If you don't want to pay some more (Aha, Mr. Heath)
Cause I'm the taxman
Yeah, I'm the taxman

Now my advice for those who die
Declare the pennies on your eyes
Cause I'm the taxman
Yeah, I'm the taxman

And you're working for no one but me
Taxman!

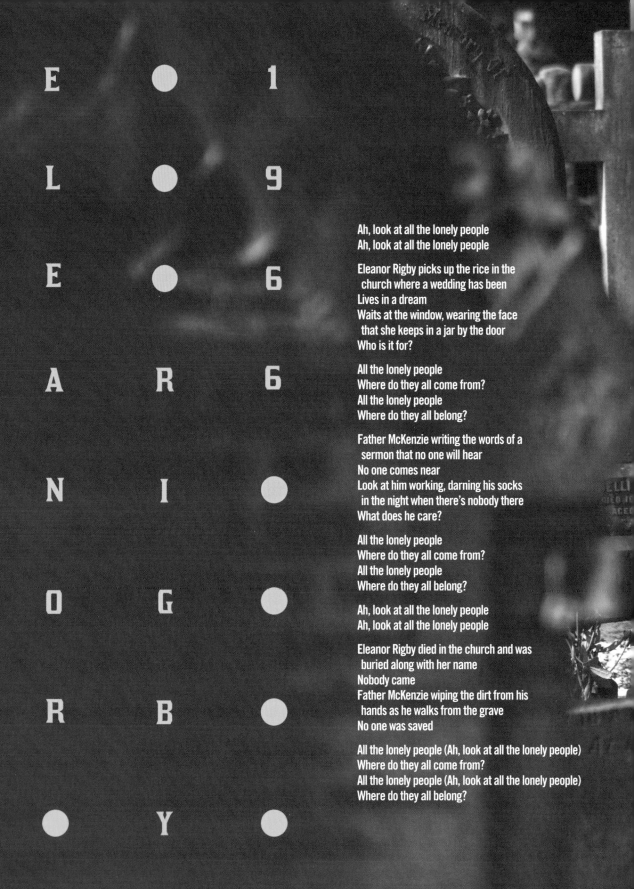

E ● 1
L ● 9
E ● 6
A R 6
N I ●
O G ●
R B ●
● Y ●

Ah, look at all the lonely people
Ah, look at all the lonely people

Eleanor Rigby picks up the rice in the
 church where a wedding has been
Lives in a dream
Waits at the window, wearing the face
 that she keeps in a jar by the door
Who is it for?

All the lonely people
Where do they all come from?
All the lonely people
Where do they all belong?

Father McKenzie writing the words of a
 sermon that no one will hear
No one comes near
Look at him working, darning his socks
 in the night when there's nobody there
What does he care?

All the lonely people
Where do they all come from?
All the lonely people
Where do they all belong?

Ah, look at all the lonely people
Ah, look at all the lonely people

Eleanor Rigby died in the church and was
 buried along with her name
Nobody came
Father McKenzie wiping the dirt from his
 hands as he walks from the grave
No one was saved

All the lonely people (Ah, look at all the lonely people)
Where do they all come from?
All the lonely people (Ah, look at all the lonely people)
Where do they all belong?

IN [...] OF

MY DEAR HUSBAND
JOHN RIGBY,
WHO DEPARTED THIS LIFE
OCT 4TH 1915 AGED 72 YEARS.
"AT REST"
ALSO FRANCES, WIFE OF THE ABOVE,
DIED APRIL 3RD 1928, AGED 85 YEARS.
ALSO DORIS W. DAUGHTER OF
F & E RIGBY, DIED DEC. 24TH 1927,
AGED 2 YEARS & 3 MONTHS.
ALSO ELEANOR RIGBY,
THE BELOVED WIFE OF THOMAS WOODS
AND GRANDDAUGHTER OF THE ABOVE
DIED 10TH OCT 1939, AGED 44 YEARS.
ASLEEP
ALSO FRANCES,
DAUGHTER OF THE ABOVE
DIED 2ND NOVEMBER 1949,
AGED 71 YEARS.

In Loving Memo[...]
THOMAS WATE[...]
THE DEARLY BELOVE[...]
THOMAS AND JANE[...]
BORN 1ST JULY [...]
DIED 23TH APRIL [...]
The Lord hath nee[...]
ALSO THE ABO[...]
THOMAS PAR[...]
WHO DIED SEPT [...]
AGED 77 YEAR[...]
"Peace, perfect [...]

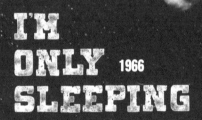

I'M ONLY
ONLY 1966
SLEEPING

When I wake up early in the morning
Lift my head, I'm still yawning
When I'm in the middle of a dream
Stay in bed, float upstream (Float upstream)
Please, don't wake me, no, don't shake me
Leave me where I am, I'm only sleeping

Everybody seems to think I'm lazy
I don't mind, I think they're crazy
Running everywhere at such a speed
Till they find there's no need (There's no need)
Please, don't spoil my day, I'm miles away
And after all I'm only sleeping

Keeping an eye on the world going by my window
Taking my time lying there and staring at the ceiling
Waiting for a sleepy feeling

Please, don't spoil my day, I'm miles away
And after all I'm only sleeping

Ooh yeah

Keeping an eye on the world going by my window
Taking my time
When I wake up early in the morning
Lift my head, I'm still yawning
When I'm in the middle of a dream
Stay in bed, float upstream (Float upstream)
Please, don't wake me, no, don't shake me
Leave me where I am,
I'm only sleeping

LOVE YOU TO

1 9 6 6

Each day just goes so fast
I turn around, it's past
You don't get time to hang a sign on me

Love me while you can
Before I'm a dead old man

A lifetime is so short
A new one can't be bought
But what you've got means such a lot to me

Make love all day long
Make love singing songs

Make love all day long
Make love singing songs

There's people standing round
Who'll screw you in the ground
They'll fill you in with all their sins, you'll see

I'll make love to you
If you want me to

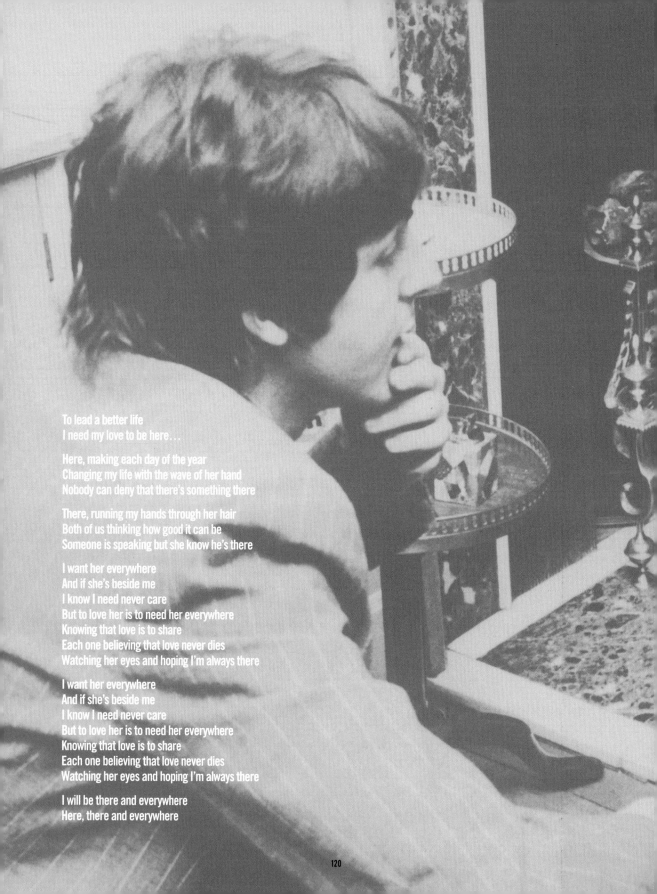

To lead a better life
I need my love to be here...

Here, making each day of the year
Changing my life with the wave of her hand
Nobody can deny that there's something there

There, running my hands through her hair
Both of us thinking how good it can be
Someone is speaking but she know he's there

I want her everywhere
And if she's beside me
I know I need never care
But to love her is to need her everywhere
Knowing that love is to share
Each one believing that love never dies
Watching her eyes and hoping I'm always there

I want her everywhere
And if she's beside me
I know I need never care
But to love her is to need her everywhere
Knowing that love is to share
Each one believing that love never dies
Watching her eyes and hoping I'm always there

I will be there and everywhere
Here, there and everywhere

HERE, THERE AND EVERYWHERE
1 9 6 6

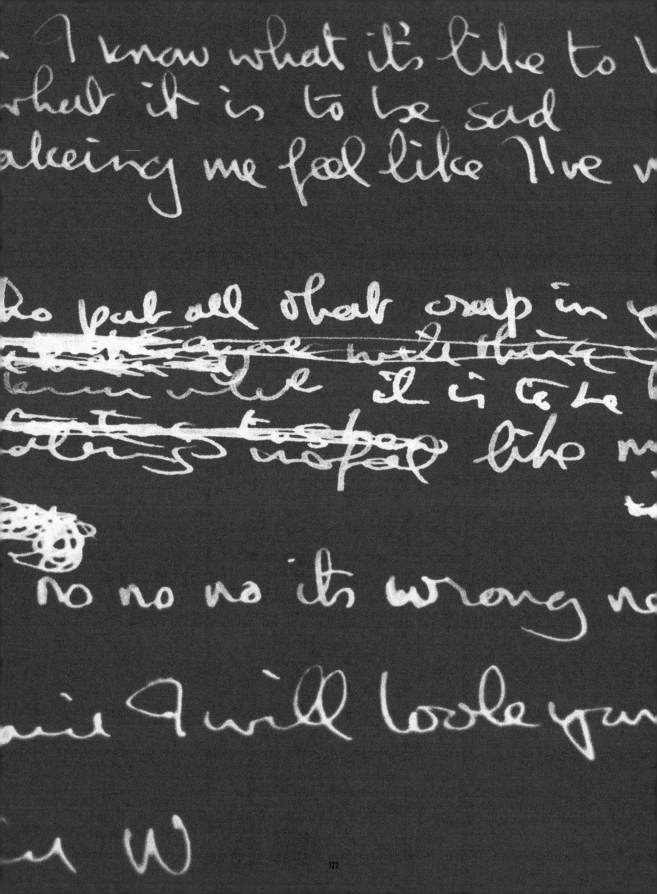

SHE SAID SHE SAID

SHE SAID SHE SAID

1966

She said "I know what it's like to be dead
I know what it is to be sad"
And she's making me feel like I've never been born

I said "Who put all those things in your head
Things that make me feel that I'm mad
And you're making me feel like I've never been born"

She said "You don't understand what I said"
I said "No, no, no, you're wrong
When I was a boy everything was right
Everything was right"

I said "Even though you know what you know
I know that I'm ready to leave
Cause you're making me feel like I've never been born"

She said "You don't understand what I said"
I said "No, no, no, you're wrong
When I was a boy everything was right
Everything was right"

I said "Even though you know what you know
I know that I'm ready to leave
Cause you're making me feel like I've never been born"

She said "I know what it's like to be dead
I know what it is to be sad
I know what it's like to be dead"

Yellow
Submarine
1966

In the town where I was born
Lived a man who sailed to sea
And he told us of his life
In the land of submarines

So we sailed on to the sun
Till we found the sea of green
And we lived beneath the waves
In our yellow submarine

We all live in a yellow submarine
Yellow submarine, yellow submarine
We all live in a yellow submarine
Yellow submarine, yellow submarine

And our friends are all aboard
Many more of them live next door
And the band begins to play

We all live in a yellow submarine
Yellow submarine, yellow submarine
We all live in a yellow submarine
Yellow submarine, yellow submarine

[Full speed ahead, Mr. Captain, full speed ahead!
Full speed over here, sir!
Action station! Action station!
Aye, aye, sir, fire!
Captain! Captain!]

As we live a life of ease (A life of ease)
Everyone of us (Everyone of us) has all we need (Has all we need)
Sky of blue (Sky of blue) and sea of green (Sea of green)
In our yellow (In our yellow) submarine (Submarine, ha, ha)

We all live in a yellow submarine
Yellow submarine, yellow submarine
We all live in a yellow submarine
Yellow submarine, yellow submarine
We all live in a yellow submarine
Yellow submarine, yellow submarine
We all live in a yellow submarine
Yellow submarine, yellow submarine

GOOD DAY SUNSHINE

1966

Good day sunshine, good day sunshine
Good day sunshine

I need to laugh and when the sun is out
I've got something I can laugh about
I feel good in a special way
I'm in love and it's a sunny day

Good day sunshine, good day sunshine
Good day sunshine

We take a walk, the sun is shining down
Burns my feet as they touch the ground

Good day sunshine, good day sunshine
Good day sunshine

Then we'd lie beneath the shady tree
I love her and she's loving me
She feels good, she knows she's looking fine
I'm so proud to know that she is mine

Good day sunshine, good day sunshine
Good day sunshine
Good day sunshine, good day sunshine
Good day sunshine
Good day sunshine, good day sunshine
Good day sunshine
Good day…

AND YOUR BIRD CAN SING 1966

You tell me that you've got everything you want
And your bird can sing
But you don't get me, you don't get me

You say you've seen seven wonders and your bird is green
But you can't see me, you can't see me

When your prized possessions
Start to weigh you down
Look in my direction
I'll be 'round, I'll be 'round

When your bird is broken will it bring you down
You may be awoken
I'll be 'round, I'll be 'round

You tell me that you've heard every sound there is
And your bird can swing
But you can't hear me, you can't hear me

DOCTOR ROBERT

1 9 6 6

Ring my friend, I said you call Doctor Robert
Day or night he'll be there any time at all, Doctor Robert
Doctor Robert, you're a new and better man
He helps you to understand
He does everything he can, Doctor Robert

If you're down he'll pick you up, Doctor Robert
Take a drink from his special cup, Doctor Robert
Doctor Robert, he's a man you must believe
Helping everyone in need
No one can succeed like Doctor Robert

Well, well, well, you're feeling fine
Well, well, well, he'll make you…
Doctor Robert

My friend works for the National Health, Doctor Robert
Don't pay money just to see yourself with Doctor Robert
Doctor Robert, you're a new and better man
He helps you to understand
He does everything he can, Doctor Robert

Well, well, well, you're feeling fine
Well, well, well, he'll make you… Doctor Robert

Ring my friend, I said you'd call Doctor Robert
Ring my friend, I said you'd call Doctor Robert
Doctor Robert

FOR NO ONE

1966

Your day breaks, your mind aches
You find that all her words of kindness linger on
When she no longer needs you

She wakes up, she makes up
She takes her time and doesn't feel she has to hurry
She no longer needs you

And in her eyes you see nothing
No sign of love behind the tears
Cried for no one
A love that should have lasted years

You want her, you need her
And yet you don't believe her when she says her love is dead
You think she needs you

And in her eyes you see nothing
No sign of love behind the tears
Cried for no one
A love that should have lasted years

You stay home, she goes out
She says that long ago she knew someone but now he's gone
She doesn't need him

Your day breaks, your mind aches
There will be times when all the things she said will fill your head
You won't forget her

And in her eyes you see nothing
No sign of love behind the tears
Cried for no one
A love that should have lasted years

GOT TO
GET YOU INTO
MY LIFE

1966

I was alone, I took a ride
I didn't know what I would find there
Another road where maybe I could see
  another kind of mind there
Ooh, then I suddenly see you
Ooh, did I tell you I need you
Every single day of my life

You didn't run, you didn't lie
You knew I wanted just to hold you
And had you gone you knew in time we'd meet again
For I had told you
Ooh, you were meant to be near me
Ooh, and I want you to hear me
Say we'll be together every day

Got to get you into my life

What can I do, what can I be
When I'm with you I want to stay there
If I'm true I'll never leave
And if I do I know the way there
Ooh, then I suddenly see you
Ooh, did I tell you I need you
Every single day of my life

Got to get you into my life
Got to get you into my life

I was alone, I took a ride
I didn't know what I would find there
Another road where maybe I could see
  another kind of mind there
Then suddenly I see you
Did I tell you I need you
Every single day of my life?

I WANT TO TELL YOU

1966

I want to tell you
My head is filled with things to say
When you're here
All those words, they seem to slip away

When I get near you
The games begin to drag me down
It's alright
I'll make you maybe next time around

But if I seem to act unkind
It's only me, it's not my mind
That is confusing things

I want to tell you
I feel hung up but I don't know why
I don't mind
I could wait forever, I've got time

Sometimes I wish I knew you well
Then I could speak my mind and tell you
Maybe you'd understand

I want to tell you
I feel hung up but I don't know why
I don't mind
I could wait forever, I've got time
I've got time, I've got time

tomorrow never knows

1966

Turn off your mind, relax and float down stream
It is not dying, it is not dying

Lay down all thought, surrender to the void
It is shining, it is shining

That you may see the meaning of within
It is being, it is being

That love is all and love is everyone
It is knowing, it is knowing

That ignorance and haste may mourn the dead
It is believing, it is believing

But listen to the colour of your dreams
It is not living, it is not living

Or play the game existence to the end
Of the beginning, of the beginning
Of the beginning, of the beginning
Of the beginning, of the beginning
Of the beginning, of the beginning

PENNY LANE 1967

In Penny Lane there is a barber showing photographs
Of every head he's had the pleasure to know
And all the people that come and go
Stop and say hello

On the corner is a banker with a motorcar
The little children laugh at him behind his back
And the banker never wears a mac in the pouring rain
Very strange

Penny Lane is in my ears and in my eyes
There beneath the blue suburban skies
I sit, and meanwhile back

In Penny Lane there is a fireman with an hourglass
And in his pocket is a portrait of the Queen
He likes to keep his fire engine clean
It's a clean machine

Penny Lane is in my ears and in my eyes
A four of fish and finger pies
In summer, meanwhile back

Behind the shelter in the middle of the roundabout
A pretty nurse is selling poppies from a tray
And though she feels as if she's in a play
She is anyway

In Penny Lane, the barber shaves another customer
We see the banker sitting waiting for a trim
And the fireman rushes in from the pouring rain
Very strange

Penny Lane is in my ears and in my eyes
There beneath the blue suburban skies
I sit and meanwhile back
Penny Lane is in my ears and in my eyes
There beneath the blue suburban skies
Penny Lane

1967 · STRAWBERRY FIELDS FOREVER

Let me take you down, cause I'm going to
Strawberry Fields
Nothing is real
And nothing to get hung about
Strawberry Fields forever

Living is easy with eyes closed
Misunderstanding all you see
It's getting hard to be someone but it all works out
It doesn't matter much to me
Let me take you down, cause I'm going to
Strawberry Fields
Nothing is real
And nothing to get hung about
Strawberry Fields forever

No one I think is in my tree
I mean it must be high or low
That is you can't, you know, tune in but it's all right
That is I think it's not too bad
Let me take you down, cause I'm going to
Strawberry Fields
Nothing is real
And nothing to get hung about
Strawberry Fields forever

Always, no sometimes, think it's me
But you know I know when it's a dream
I think I know I mean, er, yes but it's all wrong
That is I think I disagree
Let me take you down, cause I'm going to
Strawberry Fields
Nothing is real
And nothing to get hung about
Strawberry Fields forever
Strawberry Fields forever
Strawberry Fields forever

1967

It was twenty years ago today
Sgt. Pepper taught the band to play
They've been going in and out of style
But they're guaranteed to raise a smile

So may I introduce to you
The act you've known for all these years
Sgt. Pepper's Lonely Hearts Club Band

We're Sgt. Pepper's Lonely Hearts Club Band
We hope you will enjoy the show
Sgt. Pepper's Lonely Hearts Club Band
Sit back and let the evening go
Sgt. Pepper's lonely, Sgt. Pepper's lonely
Sgt. Pepper's Lonely Hearts Club Band

It's wonderful to be here
It's certainly a thrill
You're such a lovely audience
We'd like to take you home with us
We'd love to take you home

I don't really want to stop the show
But I thought that you might like to know
That the singer's going to sing a song
And he wants you all to sing along
So let me introduce to you the one and only Billy Shears
And Sgt. Pepper's Lonely Hearts Club Band

I'm fixing a hole where the rain gets in
And stops my mind from wandering
Where it will go

I'm filling the cracks that ran through the door
And kept my mind from wandering
Where it will go

And it really doesn't matter
If I'm wrong I'm right
Where I belong I'm right
Where I belong
See the people standing there
Who disagree and never win
And wonder why they don't get in my door

I'm painting the room in the colourful way
And when my mind is wandering
There I will go
Ooh ooh ooh ah ah
Hey, hey, hey, hey

And it really doesn't matter
If I'm wrong I'm right
Where I belong I'm right
Where I belong
Silly people run around
They worry me and never ask me
Why they don't get past my door

I'm taking the time for a number of things
That weren't important yesterday
And I still go
Ooh ooh ooh ah ah

I'm fixing a hole where the rain gets in
Stops my mind from wandering
Where it will go oh
Where it will go oh

I'm fixing a hole where the rain gets in
And stops my mind from wandering
Where it will go

FIXING A HOLE · 1967

With a Little Help From My Friends 1967

What would you think if I sang out of tune
Would you stand up and walk out on me?
Lend me your ears and I'll sing you a song
And I'll try not to sing out of key
Oh I get by with a little help from my friends
Mm, I get high with a little help from my friends
Mm, gonna try with a little help from my friends

What do I do when my love is away?
(Does it worry you to be alone?)
How do I feel by the end of the day?
(Are you sad because you're on your own?)
No, I get by with a little help from my friends
Mm, get high with a little help from my friends
Mm, gonna try with a little help from my friends

(Do you need anybody?)
I need somebody to love
(Could it be anybody?)
I want somebody to love

(Would you believe in a love at first sight?)
Yes I'm certain that it happens all the time
(What do you see when you turn out the light?)
I can't tell you, but I know it's mine
Oh, I get by with a little help from my friends
Mm, get high with a little help from my friends
Oh, I'm gonna try with a little help from my friends

(Do you need anybody?)
I just need someone to love
(Could it be anybody?)
I want somebody to love

Oh, I get by with a little help from my friends
Mm, gonna try with a little help from my friends
Oh, I get high with a little help from my friends
Yes, I get by with a little help from my friends
With a little help from my friends

1967

Picture yourself in a boat on a river
With tangerine trees and marmalade skies
Somebody calls you, you answer quite slowly
A girl with kaleidoscope eyes

Cellophane flowers of yellow and green
Towering over your head
Look for the girl with the sun in her eyes
And she's gone

Lucy in the sky with diamonds
Lucy in the sky with diamonds
Lucy in the sky with diamonds
Aaaaahhhhh...

Follow her down to a bridge by a fountain
Where rocking horse people eat marshmallow pies
Everyone smiles as you drift past the flowers
That grow so incredibly high

Newspaper taxis appear on the shore
Waiting to take you away
Climb in the back with your head in the clouds
And you're gone

Lucy in the sky with diamonds
Lucy in the sky with diamonds
Lucy in the sky with diamonds Aaaaahhhhh...

Picture yourself on a train in a station
With Plasticine porters with looking-glass ties
Suddenly someone is there at the turnstile
The girl with kaleidoscope eyes

Lucy in the sky with diamonds
Lucy in the sky with diamonds
Lucy in the sky with diamonds
Aaaaahhhhh...
Lucy in the sky with diamonds
Lucy in the sky with diamonds
Lucy in the sky with diamonds
Aaaaahhhhh....
Lucy in the sky with diamonds
Lucy in the sky with diamonds
Lucy in the sky with diamonds

Lucy in the Sky with Diamonds

GETTING BETTER

BETTER

1967

It's getting better all the time

I used to get mad at my school (Now I can't complain)
The teachers that taught me weren't cool (Now I can't complain)
You're holding me down (Oh)
Turning me round (Oh)
Filling me up with your rules (Foolish rules)

I've got to admit it's getting better (Better)
A little better all the time
(It can't get no worse)
I have to admit it's getting better (Better)
It's getting better since you've been mine

Me used to be angry young man
Me hiding me head in the sand
You gave me the word, I finally heard
I'm doing the best that I can

I've got to admit it's getting better (Better)
A little better all the time
(It can't get more worse)
I have to admit it's getting better (Better)
It's getting better since you've been mine

Getting so much better all the time
It's getting better all the time
Better, better, better
It's getting better all the time
Better, better, better

I used to be cruel to my woman
I beat her and kept her apart from the things that she loved
Man I was mean but I'm changing my scene
And I'm doing the best that I can (Ooh)

I admit it's getting better (Better)
A little better all the time
(It can't get more worse)
Yes I admit it's getting better (Better)
It's getting better since you've been mine
Getting so much better all the time
It's getting better all the time
Better, better, better
It's getting better all the time
Better, better, better
Getting so much better all the time

SHE'S LEAVING HOME 1967

old Melanie ... schoolgirl wh... ...med have everything, spent yes- terday searching for her in London and Brighton.

Melanie had her own car, an Austin 1100; It ... unlocked, outsid... when she vanished.

She had a wardrobe ... clothes. She took only ... she was wearing—a ... trouser suit and bla... leather shoes.

She left her cheque book and drew no money from her account.

Melanie, who has long blonde hair and is 5ft. lin. tall, was studying for her A-level ...nations. She planne... ...versity...

Wednesday morning at five o'clock as the day begins
Silently closing her bedroom door
Leaving the note that she hoped would say more
She goes downstairs to the kitchen clutching her hankerchief
Quietly turning the backdoor key
Stepping outside she is free

She (We gave her most of our lives)
Is leaving (Sacrificed most of our lives)
Home (We gave her everything money could buy)
She's leaving home after living alone
For so many years (Bye bye)

Father snores as his wife gets into her dressing gown
Picks up the letter that's lying there
Standing alone at the top of the stairs
She breaks down and cries to her husband "Daddy our baby's gone
Why would she treat us so thoughtlessly?
How could she do this to me?"

She (We never thought of ourselves)
Is leaving (Never a thought for ourselves)
Home (We struggled hard all our lives to get by)
She's leaving home after living alone
For so many years (Bye bye)

Friday morning at nine o'clock she is far away
Waiting to keep the appointment she made
Meeting a man from the motor trade

She (What did we do that was wrong)
Is having (We didn't know it was wrong)
Fun (Fun is the one thing that money can't buy)
Something inside that was always denied
For so many years (Bye bye)

She's leaving home
Bye bye

BEING FOR THE BENEFIT OF MR. KITE!
1967

For the benefit of Mr. Kite
There will be a show tonight
On trampoline
The Hendersons will all be there
Late of Pablo Fanque's Fair
What a scene!
Over men and horses hoops and garters
Lastly through a hogshead of real fire!
In this way Mr. K will challenge the world!

The celebrated Mr. K
Performs his feat on Saturday
At Bishopsgate
The Hendersons will dance and sing
As Mr. Kite flys through the ring,
Don't be late!
Messrs. K and H assure the public
Their production will be second to none
And of course Henry the Horse dances the waltz!

The band begins at ten to six
When Mr. K performs his tricks
Without a sound
And Mr. H will demonstrate
Ten somersets he'll undertake
On solid ground
Having been some days in preparation
A splendid time is guaranteed for all
And tonight Mr. Kite is topping the bill!

WITHIN YOU WITHOUT YOU

1967

We were talking about the space between us all
And the people who hide themselves behind a wall of illusion
Never glimpse the truth, then it's far too late, when they pass away
We were talking about the love we all could share
When we find it, to try our best to hold it there with our love
With our love, we could save the world, if they only knew

Try to realise it's all within yourself
No one else can make you change
And to see you're really only very small
And life flows on within you and without you

We were talking about the love that's gone so cold
And the people who gain the world and lose their soul
They don't know, they can't see, are you one of them?

When you've seen beyond yourself then you may find
Peace of mind is waiting there
And the time will come when you see we're all one
And life flows on within you and without you

WHEN I'M

1967

When I get older losing my hair	I could be handy, mending a fuse
Many years from now	When your lights have gone
Will you still be sending me a Valentine	You can knit a sweater by the fireside
Birthday greetings, bottle of wine?	Sunday mornings go for a ride
If I'd been out till quarter to three	Doing the garden, digging the weeds
Would you lock the door?	Who could ask for more?
Will you still need me, will you still feed me	Will you still need me, will you still feed me
When I'm sixty-four?	When I'm sixty-four?

You'll be older too
And if you say the word
I could stay with you

Every summer we can rent a cottage in the Isle of Wight
If it's not too dear
We shall scrimp and save
Grandchildren on your knee
Vera, Chuck & Dave

Send me a postcard, drop me a line
Stating point of view
Indicate precisely what you mean to say
Yours sincerely, wasting away
Give me your answer, fill in a form
Mine for evermore
Will you still need me, will you still feed me
When I'm sixty-four?
Ho!

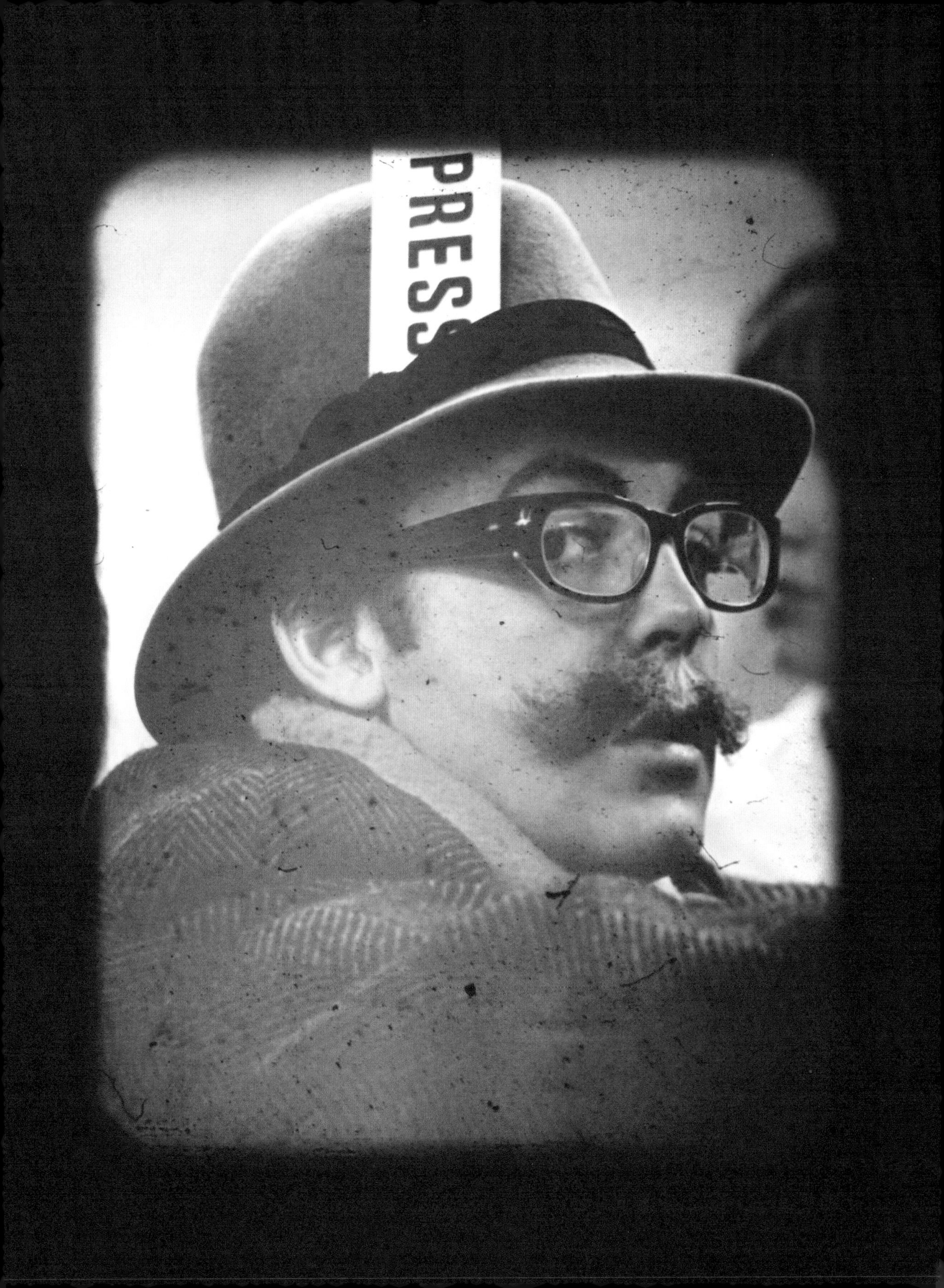
PRESS

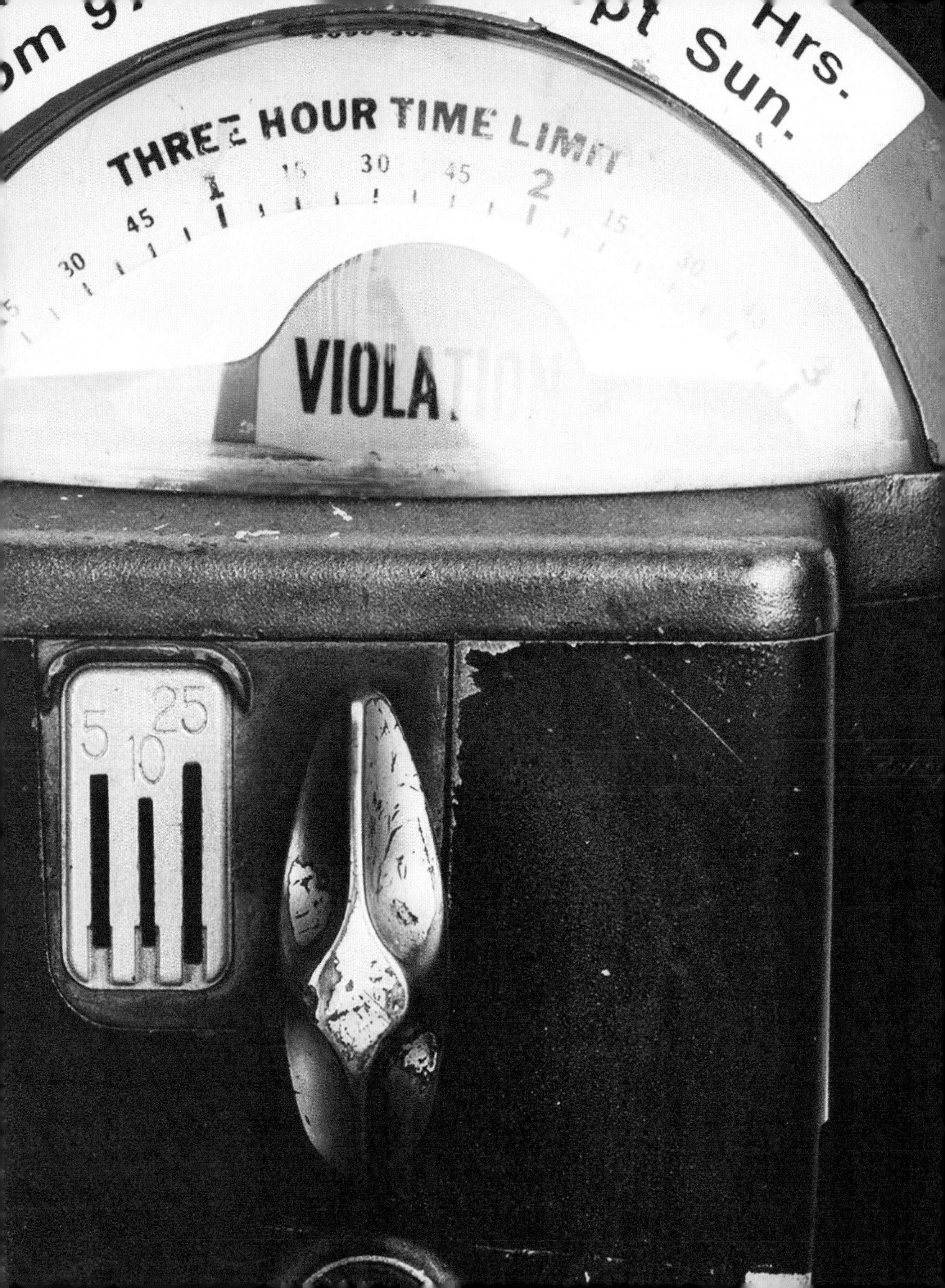

Hrs.
Sun.
HOUR TIME LIMIT
VIOLA
5 10 25

LOVELY RITA
1967

Aaaahhh…

Lovely Rita meter maid
Lovely Rita meter maid

Lovely Rita meter maid
Nothing can come between us
When it gets dark I tow your heart away
Standing by a parking meter
When I caught a glimpse of Rita
Filling in a ticket in her little white book
In a cap she looked much older
And the bag across her shoulder
Made her look a little like a military man

Lovely Rita meter maid
May I inquire discreetly (Lovely Rita)
When are you free to take some tea with me?
(Lovely Rita, maid, ah)
Rita!

Took her out and tried to win her
Had a laugh and over dinner
Told her I would really like to see her again
Got the bill and Rita paid it
Took her home I nearly made it
Sitting on the sofa with a sister or two

Oh, lovely Rita meter maid
Where would I be without you
Give us a wink and make me think of you
(Lovely Rita meter maid)
Lovely Rita meter maid, Rita meter maid
(Lovely Rita meter maid)
Oh Lovely Rita meter meter maid
(Lovely Rita meter maid)
Ah da, ah da (Lovely Rita meter maid)

GOOD MORNING
GOOD MORNING

Good morning, good morning
Good morning, good morning
Good morning ah

Nothing to do to save his life call his wife in
Nothing to say but what a day how's your boy been
Nothing to do it's up to you
I've got nothing to say but it's OK
Good morning, good morning
Good morning ah

Going to work don't want to go feeling low down
Heading for home you start to roam then you're in town
Everybody knows there's nothing doing
Everything is closed it's like a ruin
Everyone you see is half asleep
And you're on your own you're in the street

After a while you start to smile now you feel cool
Then you decide to take a walk by the old school
Nothing is changed it's still the same
I've got nothing to say but it's OK
Good morning, good morning
Good morning ah

People running round it's five o'clock
Everywhere in town is getting dark
Everyone you see is full of life
It's time for tea and Meet The Wife
Somebody needs to know the time, glad that I'm here
Watching the skirts you start to flirt now you're in gear
Go to a show you hope she goes
I've got nothing to say but it's OK

Good morning, good morning, good
Good morning, good morning, good
Good morning, good morning, good
Good morning, good morning, good
Good morning, good morning, good
Good morning, good morning, good
Good morning, good morning, good
Good morning, good morning, good
Good morning, good morning, good
Good morning, good morning, good

1967

OH BOY!

I read the news today oh boy
About a lucky man who made the grade
And though the news was rather sad
Well I just had to laugh
I saw the photograph
He blew his mind out in a car
He didn't notice that the lights had changed
A crowd of people stood and stared
They'd seen his face before
Nobody was really sure
If he was from the House of Lords

I saw a film today oh boy
The English Army had just won the war
A crowd of people turned away
But I just had to look
Having read the book
I'd love to turn you on

Woke up, fell out of bed
Dragged a comb across my head
Found my way downstairs and drank a cup
And looking up I noticed I was late
Found my coat and grabbed my hat
Made the bus in seconds flat
Found my way upstairs and had a smoke
And somebody spoke
and I went into a dream

I read the news today oh boy
Four thousand holes in Blackburn, Lancashire
And though the holes were rather small
They had to count them all
Now they know how many holes it takes to fill the Albert Hall
I'd love to turn you on

1967

Love, love, love
Love, love, love
Love, love, love

There's nothing you can do that can't be done
Nothing you can sing that can't be sung
Nothing you can say but you can learn how to play the game
It's easy

Nothing you can make that can't be made
No one you can save that can't be saved
Nothing you can do but you can learn how to be you in time
It's easy

All you need is love
All you need is love
All you need is love, love
Love is all you need

Love, love, love
Love, love, love
Love, love, love

All you need is love
All you need is love
All you need is love, love
Love is all you need

Nothing you can know that isn't known
Nothing you can see that isn't shown
Nowhere you can be that isn't where you're meant to be
It's easy

All you need is love
All you need is love
All you need is love, love
Love is all you need

All you need is love (All together, now!)
All you need is love (Everybody!)
All you need is love, love
Love is all you need
Love is all you need (Love is all you need)
Love is all you need (Love is all you need)
Love is all you need (Love is all you need)
Love is all you need (Love is all you need)
Love is all you need (Love is all you need)
Love is all you need (Love is all you need)
Love is all you need (Love is all you need)
Love is all you need (Love is all you need)
Love is all you need (Love is all you need)
Love is all you need (Love is all you need)
Yee-hai! (Love is all you need)
Love is all you need (Love is all you need)
Love is all you need (Love is all you need)
Love is all you need (Love is all you need)
Oh yeah! (Love is all you need)
She loves you, yeah yeah yeah
(Love is all you need)
She loves you, yeah yeah yeah
(Love is all you need)

HELLO GOODBYE
1967

You say yes, I say no
You say stop and I say go go go, oh, oh no
You say goodbye and I say hello
Hello hello
I don't know why you say goodbye, I say hello
Hello hello
I don't know why you say goodbye, I say hello

I say high, you say low
You say why and I say I don't know, oh, oh no
You say goodbye and I say hello
(Hello goodbye hello goodbye) Hello hello
(Hello goodbye) I don't know why you say goodbye
 I say hello
(Hello goodbye hello goodbye) Hello hello
(Hello goodbye) I don't know why you say goodbye
(Hello goodbye) I say hello/goodbye

Why why why why why why do you say
goodbye goodbye, oh no?

You say goodbye and I say hello
Hello hello
I don't know why you say goodbye, I say hello
Hello hello
I don't know why you say goodbye, I say hello

You say yes (I say yes) I say no (But I may mean no)
You say stop (I can stay) and I say go go go
(Till it's time to go), oh
Oh no
You say goodbye and I say hello
Hello hello
I don't know why you say goodbye, I say hello
Hello hello
I don't know why you say goodbye, I say hello
Hello hello
I don't know why you say goodbye, I say hello
Hello

Heyla heba helloa
Heyla heba helloa
Heyla heba helloa

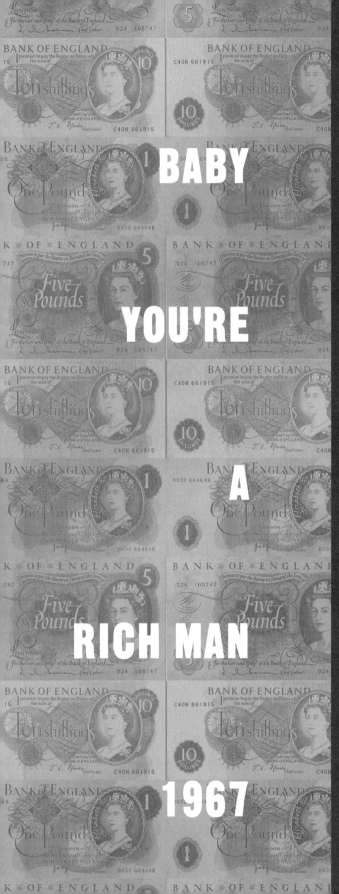

BABY YOU'RE A RICH MAN

1967

How does it feel to be
One of the beautiful people?
Now that you know who you are
What do you want to be?
And have you travelled very far?
Far as the eye can see

How does it feel to be
One of the beautiful people?
How often have you been there?
Often enough to know
What did you see when you were there?
Nothing that doesn't show
Baby you're a rich man
Baby you're a rich man
Baby you're a rich man too
You keep all your money in a big brown bag inside a zoo
What a thing to do
Baby you're a rich man
Baby you're a rich man
Baby you're a rich man too

How does it feel to be
One of the beautiful people?
Tuned to a natural E
Happy to be that way
Now that you've found another key What are you going to play?
Baby you're a rich man
Baby you're a rich man
Baby you're a rich man too
You keep all your money in a big brown bag inside a zoo
What a thing to do
Baby, baby you're a rich man
Baby you're a rich man
Baby you're a rich man too
Baby you're a rich man
Baby you're a rich man
Baby, baby you're a rich man too

ONLY A NORTHERN SONG

by JOHN LENNON and PAUL McCARTNEY   1969

Recorded by THE BEATLES on PARLOPHONE

If you're listening to this song
You may think the chords are going wrong
But they're not
He just wrote it like that

When you're listening late at night
You may think the band are not quite right
But they are
They just play it like that

It doesn't really matter what chords I play
What words I say or time of day it is
As it's only a Northern Song

It doesn't really matter what clothes I wear
Or how I fare or if my hair is brown
When it's only a Northern song

If you think the harmony
Is a little dark and out of key
You're correct
There's nobody there

And I told you there's no one there

NORTHERN SONGS LTD
132 CHARING CROSS ROAD, LONDON, W.C.2.

2/6

ALL NOW

TOGETHER

1969

One, two, three, four
Can I have a little more?
Five, six, seven, eight, nine, ten
I love you

A, B, C, D
Can I bring my friend to tea?
E, F, G, H, I, J, I love you

(Boom boom boom boom-ba-boom)
Sail the ship
(Boom-ba-boom) Chop the tree
(Boom-ba-boom) Skip the rope
(Boom-ba-boom) Look at me

(All together now) All together now
(All together now) All together now
(All together now) All together now
(All together now) All together now

Black, white, green, red
Can I take my friend to bed?
Pink, brown, yellow, orange and blue
I love you

(All together now) All together now
(All together now) All together now
(All together now) All together now
(All together now) All together now
(All together now) All together now
(All together now) All together now
(All together now) All together now
(All together now) All together now
(All together now) All together now

(Boom boom boom boom-ba-boom)
Sail the ship
(Boom boom boom boom-ba-boom)
Chop the tree
(Boom boom boom boom-ba-boom)
Skip the rope
(Boom-ba-boom) Look at me

(All together now), All together now
(All together now), All together now
(All together now), All together now
(All together now), All together now
(All together now), All together now
(All together now), All together now
(All together now), All together now
(All together now), All together now
(All together now), All together now
(All together now), All together now
(All together now), All together now
(All together now), All together now

IT'S ALL TOO MUCH

1969

It's all too much
It's all too much

When I look into your eyes
Your love is there for me
And the more I go inside
The more there is to see

It's all too much for me to take
The love that's shining all around you
Everywhere, it's what you make
For us to take, it's all too much

Floating down the stream of time
From life to life with me
Makes no difference where you are
Or where you'd like to be

It's all too much for me to take
The love that's shining all around here
All the world is birthday cake
So take a piece but not too much

Sail me on a silver sun
Where I know that I'm free
Show me that I'm everywhere
And get me home for tea

It's all too much for me to see
The love that's shining all around here
The more I learn, the less I know
But what I do is all too much

It's all too much for me to take
The love that's shining all around you
Everywhere, it's what you make
For us to take, it's all too much

It's too much
Ah, it's too much

With your long blond hair and your eyes of blue
With your long blond hair and your eyes of blue

You're too much, ah
We are getting in touch

Too much, too much, too much
Too much, too much, too much
Too much, too much, too much
Too much, too much, too much
Too much, too much, too much
Too much, too much, too much
Too much, too much, too much
Too much, too much, too much
Too much

Much, much, much, much, much
Much, much, much, much, much
Much, much, much, much, much
Much, much, much, much, much
Much, much, much, much, much

Sheepdog
Standing in the rain
Bullfrog
Doing it again
Some kind of happiness is measured out in miles
What makes you think you're something special when you smile?

Child-like
No one understands
Jack knife
In your sweaty hands
Some kind of innocence is measured out in years
You don't know what it's like to listen to your fears

You can talk to me
You can talk to me
You can talk to me,
If you're lonely you can talk to me

Big man (Yeah)
Walking in the park
Wigwam
Frightened of the dark
Some kind of solitude is measured out in you
You think you know me but you haven't got a clue

You can talk to me
You can talk to me
You can talk to me,
If you're lonely you can talk to me
Hey!

Wahoo woof! Woof!

Hey bulldog! Woof! Hey bulldog!
Hey bulldog! Hey bulldog!

[Hey man, what's that noise?

Woof!

What d'you say?

I said woof!

D'you know anymore?

Wooaah ha ha ha!

You got it. That's it. You're brilliant. That's it, man. That's it.
You've got it

Don't look at me, man. I only have grandchildren.

Ah ho! Ha ha ha ha ha ha!

Quiet boy, quiet!
OK.]

Hey bulldog!
Hey bulldog!

HEY
1969
BULLDOG

1967

There's a fog upon L.A.
And my friends have lost their way
"We'll be over soon," they said
Now they've lost themselves instead
Please don't be long
Please don't you be very long
Please don't be long for I may be asleep

Well it only goes to show
And I told them where to go
Ask a policeman on the street
There's so many there to meet
Please don't be long
Please don't you be very long
Please don't be long for I may be asleep

Now it's past my bed I know
And I'd really like to go
Soon will be the break of day
Sitting here in Blue Jay Way

Please don't be long
Please don't you be very long
Please don't be long for I may be asleep

Please don't be long
Please don't you be very long
Please don't be long
Please don't be long
Please don't you be very long
Please don't be long
Please don't be long
Please don't you be very long

Please don't be long
Don't be long, don't be long, don't be long
Don't be long, don't be long, don't be long

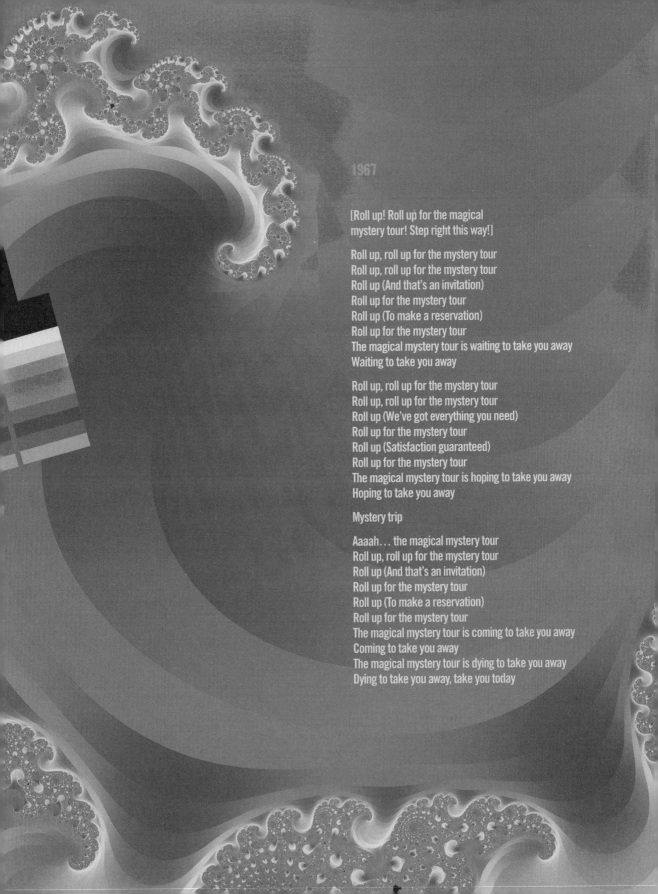

1967

[Roll up! Roll up for the magical
mystery tour! Step right this way!]

Roll up, roll up for the mystery tour
Roll up, roll up for the mystery tour
Roll up (And that's an invitation)
Roll up for the mystery tour
Roll up (To make a reservation)
Roll up for the mystery tour
The magical mystery tour is waiting to take you away
Waiting to take you away

Roll up, roll up for the mystery tour
Roll up, roll up for the mystery tour
Roll up (We've got everything you need)
Roll up for the mystery tour
Roll up (Satisfaction guaranteed)
Roll up for the mystery tour
The magical mystery tour is hoping to take you away
Hoping to take you away

Mystery trip

Aaaah. . . the magical mystery tour
Roll up, roll up for the mystery tour
Roll up (And that's an invitation)
Roll up for the mystery tour
Roll up (To make a reservation)
Roll up for the mystery tour
The magical mystery tour is coming to take you away
Coming to take you away
The magical mystery tour is dying to take you away
Dying to take you away, take you today

THE FOOL ON THE HILL

1967

Day after day, alone on a hill
The man with the foolish grin
 is keeping perfectly still
But nobody wants to know him
They can see that he's just a fool
And he never gives an answer

But the fool on the hill
Sees the sun going down
And the eyes in his head
See the world spinning around

Well on the way, head in a cloud
The man of a thousand voices talking
 perfectly loud
But nobody ever hears him
Or the sound he appears to make
And he never seems to notice

But the fool on the hill
Sees the sun going down
And the eyes in his head
See the world spinning around

And nobody seems to like him
They can tell what he wants to do
And he never shows his feelings

But the fool on the hill
Sees the sun going down
And the eyes in his head
See the world spinning around

He never listens to them
He knows that they're the fools
They don't like him

The fool on the hill
Sees the sun going down
And the eyes in his head
See the world spinning around

Your Mother Should Know

1967

Let's all get up and dance to a song
That was a hit before your mother was born
Though she was born a long, long time ago
Your mother should know
(Your mother should...)
Your mother should know (...yeah)
Sing it again
Let's all get up and dance to a song
That was a hit before your mother was born
Though she was born a long, long time ago
Your mother should know
(Your mother should...)
Your mother should know (... yeah)

Lift up your hearts and sing me a song
That was a hit before your mother was born
Though she was born a long, long time ago
Your mother should know
(Your mother... yeah)
Your mother should know (... aaaaah)
Your mother should know
(Your mother should...)
Your mother should know (... aaaaah)

Sing it again
Da da da da...
Though she was born a long, long time ago
Your mother should know
(Your mother should...)
Your mother should know (... yeah)
Your mother should know
(Your mother should...)
Your mother should know (... yeah)
Your mother should know
(Your mother should...)
Your mother should know (... yeah)

I AM THE WALRUS

WALRUS

1967

I am he as you are he as you are me
And we are all together
See how they run like pigs from a gun
See how they fly
I'm crying

Sitting on a cornflake
Waiting for the van to come
Corporation tee shirt
Stupid bloody Tuesday
Man you been a naughty boy
You let your face grow long

I am the eggman, they are the eggmen
I am the walrus, goo goo g' joob

Mister City Policeman sitting,
Pretty little policemen in a row
See how they fly like Lucy in the sky
See how they run
I'm crying, I'm crying
I'm crying, I'm crying

Yellow matter custard
Dripping from a dead dog's eye
Crabalocker fishwife
Pornographic priestess
Boy you been a naughty girl
You let your knickers down

I am the eggman, they are the eggmen
I am the walrus, goo goo g' joob

Sitting in an English garden
Waiting for the sun
If the sun don't come
You get a tan from standing in the
English rain

I am the eggman, they are the eggmen
I am the walrus, goo goo g' joob goo
goo goo g' joob

Expert texpert choking smokers
Don't you think the joker laughs at you?
(Ho ho ho! He he he! Ha ha ha!)
See how they smile like pigs in a sty
See how they snied
I'm crying

Semolina pilchard
Climbing up the Eiffel Tower
Elementary penguin singing Hare Krishna
Man you should have seen them
Kicking Edgar Allan Poe

I am the eggman, they are the eggmen
I am the walrus, goo goo g' joob goo goo g' joob
Goo goo g' joob goo goo g' joob
Goo goooooooooo jooba jooba jooba
jooba jooba jooba
Jooba jooba
Jooba jooba
Jooba joob

Oompah oompah, stick it up your jumper
Everybody's got one

["Slave, thou has slain me;
Villain, take my purse
If ever thou wilt thrive, bury my body
And give the letters which thou find'st about me
To Edmund Earl of Gloster; seek him out
Upon the British party: O, untimely death"

"I know thee well: a serviceable villain;
As duteous to the vices of thy mistress
As badness would desire."

"What, is he dead?"

"Sit you down, father; rest you."]

[Extract from Shakespeare's *King Lear*, Act 4, Scene 6
that John taped from the radio.]

LADY MADONNA 1968

Lady Madonna, children at your feet
Wonder how you manage to make ends meet
Who finds the money when you pay the rent?
Did you think that money was Heaven sent?

Friday night arrives without a suitcase
Sunday morning creeping like a nun
Monday's child has learned to tie his bootlace
See how they run

Lady Madonna, baby at your breast
Wonders how you manage to feed the rest

See how they run

Lady Madonna, lying on the bed
Listen to the music playing in your head

Tuesday afternoon is never ending
Wednesday morning papers didn't come
Thursday night your stockings needed mending
See how they run

Lady Madonna, children at your feet
Wonder how you manage to make ends meet

THE INNER LIGHT

1968

Without going out of my door
I can know all things on Earth
Without looking out of my window
I could know the ways of Heaven

The farther one travels
The less one knows
The less one really knows

Without going out of your door
You can know all things on Earth
Without looking out of your window
You could know the ways of Heaven

The farther one travels
The less one knows
The less one really knows

Arrive without travelling
See all without looking
Do all without doing

HEY JUDE

1968

Words and Music by
JOHN LENNON and PAUL McCARTNEY

Hey Jude, don't make it bad
Take a sad song and make it better
Remember to let her into your heart
Then you can start to make it better

Hey Jude, don't be afraid
You were made to go out and get her
The minute you let her under your skin
Then you begin to make it better

And anytime you feel the pain, hey Jude, refrain
Don't carry the world upon your shoulders
For well you know that it's a fool who plays it cool
By making his world a little colder
Nah nah nah nah nah nah nah nah nah

Hey Jude, don't let me down
You have found her, now go and get her
Remember to let her into your heart
Then you can start to make it better

So let it out and let it in, hey Jude, begin
You're waiting for someone to perform with
And don't you know that it's just you
Hey Jude, you'll do
The movement you need is on your shoulder
Nah nah nah nah nah nah nah nah nah yeah

Hey Jude, don't make it bad
Take a sad song and make it better
Remember to let her under your skin
Then you'll begin to make it
Better better better better better better,
Oh

Nah nah nah nah nah nah, nah nah nah,
Hey Jude
Nah nah nah nah nah nah, nah nah nah,
Hey Jude
Nah nah nah nah nah nah, nah nah nah,
Hey Jude
Nah nah nah nah nah nah, nah nah nah,
Hey Jude
Nah nah nah nah nah nah, nah nah nah,
Hey Jude
Nah nah nah nah nah nah, nah nah nah,
Hey Jude
Nah nah nah nah nah nah, nah nah nah,
Hey Jude
Nah nah nah nah nah nah, nah nah nah,
Hey Jude
Nah nah nah nah nah nah, nah nah nah,
Hey Jude
Nah nah nah nah nah nah, nah nah nah,
Hey Jude
Nah nah nah nah nah nah, nah nah nah,
Hey Jude
Nah nah nah nah nah nah, nah nah nah,
Hey Jude
Nah nah nah nah nah nah, nah nah nah,
Hey Jude
Nah nah nah nah nah nah, nah nah nah,
Hey Jude
Nah nah nah nah nah nah, nah nah nah,
Hey Jude
Nah nah nah nah nah nah, nah nah nah,
Hey Jude

MACLEN MUSIC, INC.
from the
ATV MUSIC GROUP

① Hey Jude dont make it bad.

BREAK

② Hey Jude dont be afraid.

---(middle)— and any time you feel the pain

③ Hey Jude dont let me down.
    ---- better, better, better BREAK.

----(Middle) let it out + let it in ...

④ Hey Jude dont make it bad.

better. better, better BREAK

        Ending. fading

BACK IN T

Oh, flew in from Miami Beach B.O.A.C.
Didn't get to bed last night
On the way the paper bag was on my knee
Man I had a dreadful flight
I'm back in the U.S.S.R.
You don't know how lucky you are boy
Back in the U.S.S.R.

Been away so long I hardly knew the place
Gee it's good to be back home
Leave it till tomorrow to unpack my case
Honey disconnect the phone
I'm back in the U.S.S.R.
You don't know how lucky you are boy

Back in the U.S.
Back in the U.S.
Back in the U.S.S.R.

Well the Ukraine girls really knock me out
They leave the West behind
And Moscow girls make me sing and shout
That Georgia's always on my my my my my my mind

Aw come on!
Ho yeah!
Ho yeah!
Ho ho yeah!
Yeah yeah!

НС U.S.S.R

Yeah I'm back in the U.S.S.R.
You don't know how lucky you are boys
Back in the U.S.S.R.

Well the Ukraine girls really knock me out
They leave the West behind
And Moscow girls make me sing and shout
That Georgia's always on my my my my my my mind

Oh, show me around the snow-peaked mountains way down south
Take me to your daddy's farm
Let me hear your balalaikas ringing out
Come and keep your comrade warm
I'm back in the U.S.S.R.
Hey you don't know how lucky you are boys
Back in the U.S.S.R.

Oh let me tell you, honey
Hey, I'm back!
I'm back in the U.S.S.R.
Yes, I'm free!
Yeah, back in the U.S.S.R.

DEAR PRUDENCE

1968

Dear Prudence
Won't you come out to play?
Dear Prudence, greet the brand new day
The sun is up, the sky is blue
It's beautiful and so are you
Dear Prudence
Won't you come out to play?

Dear Prudence, open up your eyes
Dear Prudence, see the sunny skies
The wind is low, the birds will sing
That you are part of everything
Dear Prudence
Won't you open up your eyes?

Look around round {round round round
round round round round round)
Look around round {round round round round
round round round round)
Look around (ah, ah, ah, ah)

Dear Prudence, let me see you smile
Dear Prudence, like a little child
The clouds will be a daisy chain
So let me see you smile again
Dear Prudence
Won't you let me see you smile?

Dear Prudence,
Won't you come out to play?
Dear Prudence, greet the brand new day
The sun is up, the sky is blue
It's beautiful and so are you
Dear Prudence
Won't you come out to play?

G L A S S   O N I O N

1 9 6 8

I told you about Strawberry Fields
You know the place where nothing is real
Well here's another place you can go
Where everything flows
Looking through the bent backed tulips
To see how the other half live
Looking through a glass onion

I told you about the walrus and me, man
You know that we're as close as can be, man
Well here's another clue for you all
The walrus was Paul
Standing on the Cast Iron Shore, yeah
Lady Madonna trying to make ends meet, yeah

Looking through a glass onion

Oh yeah
Oh yeah
Oh yeah
Looking through a glass onion

I told you 'bout the fool on the hill
I tell you man he living there still
Well here's another place you can be
Listen to me
Fixing a hole in the ocean
Trying to make a dovetail joint, yeah
Looking through a glass onion

Desmond has his barrow in the market place
Molly is the singer in a band
Desmond says to Molly "Girl I like your face"
And Molly says this as she takes him by the hand

Ob-la-di ob-la-da life goes on bra
La-la how the life goes on
Ob-la-di ob-la-da life goes on bra
La-la how the life goes on

Desmond takes a trolley to the jeweller's store
Buys a twenty carat golden ring (ring)
Takes it back to Molly waiting at the door
And as he gives it to her she begins to sing (sing)

Ob-la-di ob-la-da life goes on bra
La-la how the life goes on
Ob-la-di ob-la-da life goes on bra
La-la how the life goes on, yeah

In a couple of years they have built
A home sweet home
With a couple of kids running in the yard
Of Desmond and Molly Jones
(Ah ha ha ha ha ha)

Happy ever after in the market place
Desmond lets the children lend a hand
(Arm! Leg!)
Molly stays at home and does her pretty face
And in the evening she still sings it with the band

Yes, ob-la-di ob-la-da life goes on bra
La-la how the life goes on (Ha ha ha)
Hey, ob-la-di ob-la-da life goes on bra
La-la how the life goes on

In a couple of years they have built
A home sweet home
With a couple of kids running in the yard
Of Desmond and Molly Jones
(Ha ha ha ha ha ha ha ha ha ha)

Yeah, happy ever after in the market place
Molly lets the children lend a hand
Desmond stays at home and does his pretty face
And in the evening she's a singer with the band

Yeah, ob-la-di ob-la-da life goes on bra
La-la how the life goes on
Yeah, ob-la-di ob-la-da life goes on bra
La-la how the life goes on

And if you want some fun
Take ob-la-di ob-la-da

MARTHA MY DEAR

1968

Martha my dear though I spend my days in conversation
Please
Remember me Martha my love
Don't forget me Martha my dear

Hold your head up you silly girl look what you've done
When you find yourself in the thick of it
Help yourself to a bit of what is all around you
Silly girl

Take a good look around you
Take a good look you're bound to see
That you and me were meant to be for each other
Silly girl

Hold your hand out you silly girl see what you've done
When you find yourself in the thick of it
Help yourself to a bit of what is all around you
Silly girl

Martha my dear you have always been my inspiration
Please
Be good to me Martha my love
Don't forget me Martha my dear

WILD HONEY PIE

1968

Honey Pie
Honey Pie

Honey Pie
Honey Pie

Honey Pie
Honey Pie
Honey Pie
Honey Pie

I Love you

THE CONTINUING STORY OF BUNGALOW BILL 1968

Hey, Bungalow Bill, what did you kill, Bungalow Bill?
Hey, Bungalow Bill, what did you kill, Bungalow Bill?

He went out tiger hunting with his elephant and gun
In case of accidents he always took his mom
He's the all American bullet-headed Saxon mother's son
All the children sing

Hey, Bungalow Bill, what did you kill, Bungalow Bill?
Hey, Bungalow Bill, what did you kill, Bungalow Bill?

Deep in the jungle where the mighty tiger lies
Bill and his elephants were taken by surprise
So Captain Marvel zapped him right between the eyes, ZAP!
All the children sing

Hey, Bungalow Bill, what did you kill, Bungalow Bill?
Hey, Bungalow Bill, what did you kill, Bungalow Bill?

The children asked him if to kill was not a sin
"Not when he looked so fierce," his mummy butted in
If looks could kill it would have been us instead of him
All the children sing

Hey, Bungalow Bill, what did you kill, Bungalow Bill?
Hey, Bungalow Bill, what did you kill, Bungalow Bill?

Oh ho!

Hey, Bungalow Bill, what did you kill, Bungalow Bill?
Hey, Bungalow Bill, what did you kill, Bungalow Bill?
Hey, Bungalow Bill, what did you kill, Bungalow Bill?
Hey, Bungalow Bill, what did you kill, Bungalow Bill?
Hey, Bungalow Bill, what did you kill, Bungalow Bill?
Hey, Bungalow Bill, what did you kill,Bungalow Bill?
[Eh up!]

HAPPINESS IS A WARM GUN

1968

She's not a girl who misses much
Do do do do do do do do, oh yeah
She's well acquainted with the touch of the velvet hand
Like a lizard on a window pane
The man in the crowd with the multicoloured mirrors
On his hobnail boots
Lying with his eyes while his hands are busy working overtime
A soap impression of his wife which he ate and donated to the National Trust

Down
I need a fix cause I'm going down
Down to the bits that I left uptown
I need a fix cause I'm going down

Mother Superior jump the gun
Mother Superior jump the gun
Mother Superior jump the gun
Mother Superior jump the gun
Mother Superior jump the gun
Mother Superior jump the gun

Happiness is a warm gun
(Happiness bang, bang, shoot, shoot)
Happiness is a warm gun, mama
(Happiness bang, bang, shoot, shoot)
When I hold you in my arms (Oo-oo oh yeah)
And I feel my finger on your trigger (Oo-oo oh yeah)
I know nobody can do me no harm (Oo-oo oh yeah)

Because happiness is a warm gun, mama
(Happiness bang, bang, shoot, shoot)
Happiness is a warm gun, yes it is
(Happiness bang, bang, shoot, shoot)
Happiness is a warm, yes it is, gun
(Happiness bang, bang, shoot, shoot)
Well, don't you know happiness is a warm gun, mama?
(Happiness is a warm gun, yeah)

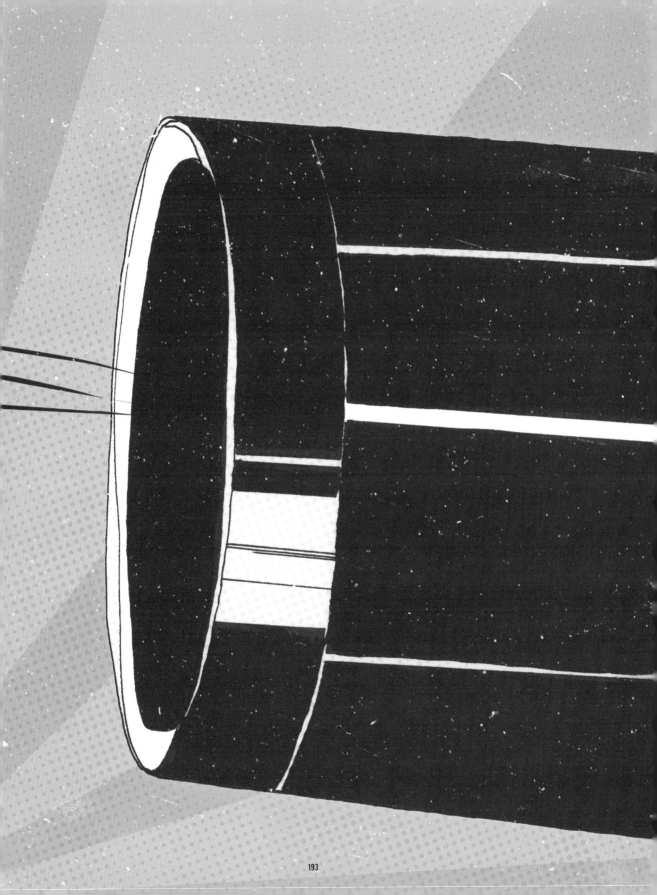

I'm so tired 1968

I'm so tired, I haven't slept a wink
I'm so tired, my mind is on the blink
I wonder should I get up
And fix myself a drink
No, no, no

I'm so tired I don't know what to do
I'm so tired my mind is set on you
I wonder should I call you
But I know what you would do

You'd say I'm putting you on
But it's no joke, it's doing me harm
You know I can't sleep
I can't stop my brain
You know it's three weeks
I'm going insane
You know I'd give you everything I've got
For a little peace of mind

I'm so tired, I'm feeling so upset
Although I'm so tired
I'll have another cigarette
And curse Sir Walter Raleigh
He was such a stupid git

You'd say I'm putting you on
But it's no joke, it's doing me harm
You know I can't sleep
I can't stop my brain
You know it's three weeks
I'm going insane
You know I'd give you everything I've got
For a little peace of mind
I'd give you everything I've got
For a little peace of mind
I'd give you everything I've got
For a little peace of mind

BLACKBIRD

1968

Blackbird singing in the dead of night
Take these broken wings and learn to fly
All your life
You were only waiting for this moment to arise

Blackbird singing in the dead of night
Take these sunken eyes and learn to see
All your life
You were only waiting for this moment to be free

Blackbird fly Blackbird fly
Into the light of the dark black night

Blackbird fly
Blackbird fly
Into the light of the dark black night

Blackbird singing in the dead of night
Take these broken wings and learn to fly
All your life
You were only waiting for this moment to arise
You were only waiting for this moment to arise
You were only waiting for this moment to arise

ROCKY R

1968

Now somewhere in the black mountain hills of Dakota
There lived a young boy named Rocky Raccoon
And one day his woman ran off with another guy
Hit young Rocky in the eye Rocky didn't like that
He said "I'm gonna get that boy"
So one day he walked into town
Booked himself a room in the local saloon

Rocky Raccoon checked into his room
Only to find Gideon's Bible
Rocky had come equipped with a gun
To shoot off the legs of his rival

His rival it seems had broken his dreams
By stealing the girl of his fancy
Her name was Magil and she called herself Lil
But everyone knew her as Nancy

Now she and her man who called himself Dan
Were in the next room at the hoedown
Rocky burst in and grinning a grin
He said "Danny boy this is a showdown"
But Daniel was hot, he drew first and shot
And Rocky collapsed in the corner, ah

D'da d'da d'da da da da
D'da d'da d'da da da da
D'da d'da d'da da d'da d'da d'da d'da
Do do do do do do

D'do d'do d'do do do do
D'do d'do d'do do do do
D'do d'do d'do do do do d'do d'do d'do
d'do
Do do do do do do

Now the doctor came in stinking of gin
And proceeded to lie on the table
He said "Rocky you met your match"
And Rocky said "Doc it's only a scratch,
And I'll be better, I'll be better Doc as soon as I am able"

And now Rocky Raccoon
He fell back in his room
Only to find Gideon's bible
Gideon checked out
And he left it no doubt
To help with good Rocky's revival, ah
Oh yeah, yeah

D'do d'do d'do do do do
D'do d'do d'do do do do
D'do d'do d'do do do do d'do d'do d'do
d'do
Do do do do do do

D'do d'do d'do do do do,
Come on, Rocky boy
D'do d'do d'do do do do,
Come on, Rocky boy
D'do d'do d'do do do do d'do d'do d'do d'do
The story of Rocky there

WHY DON'T WE DO IT IN THE ROAD?

1968

Why don't we d-do it in the road? Mm
Why don't we do it in the road? Ah
Why don't we d-do it, do it in the road?
Mm
Why don't we do it in the road? Mm
No one will be watching us
Why don't we do it in the road?

Why don't we do it in the road?
Why don't we do it in the road?
Why don't we do it in the road?
Why don't we do it in the road?
No one will be watching us
Why don't we do it in the road?

Ooh

Why don't we do it in the road?
Why don't we do it in the road?
Why don't we do it, do it in the road?
 Why don't we do it in the road?
No one will be watching us
Why don't we do it in the road?

I WILL

1968

Who knows how long I've loved you
You know I love you still
Will I wait a lonely lifetime
If you want me to, I will

For if I ever saw you
I didn't catch your name
But it never really mattered
I will always feel the same

Love you forever and forever
Love you with all my heart
Love you whenever we're together
Love you when we're apart

And when at last I find you
Your song will fill the air
Sing it loud so I can hear you
Make it easy to be near you
For the things you do endear you
to me
Oh, you know I will
I will

Mm mm mm mm mm mm mm mm mm
Da da da da da da da

JULIA

1968

Half of what I say is meaningless
But I say it just to reach you, Julia

Julia, Julia, oceanchild, calls me
So I sing a song of love, Julia
Julia, seashell eyes, windy smile, calls me
So I sing a song of love, Julia

Her hair of floating sky is shimmering
Glimmering
In the sun

Julia, Julia, morning moon, touch me
So I sing a song of love, Julia

When I cannot sing my heart
I can only speak my mind, Julia
Julia, sleeping sand, silent cloud, touch me
So I sing a song of love, Julia
Mmm mm mm mm… calls me
So I sing a song of love for Julia, Julia, Julia

BIRTHDAY
1968

They say it's your birthday
It's my birthday too, yeah
They say it's your birthday
We're gonna have a good time
I'm glad it's your birthday
Happy birthday to you

Dance, dance, dance
Come on, come on

Yes we're going to a party party
Yes we're going to a party party
Yes we're going to a party party

I would like you to dance (Birthday)
Take a cha-cha-cha-chance (Birthday)
I would like you to dance (Birthday)
Dance yeah

Oh
Come on

I would like you to dance (Birthday)
Take a cha-cha-cha-chance (Birthday)
I would like you to dance (Birthday)
Oh dance! Dance

They say it's your birthday
Well it's my birthday too, yeah
They say it's your birthday
We're gonna have a good time
I'm glad it's your birthday
Happy birthday to you

2, 3

Yes I'm lonely wanna die
Yes I'm lonely wanna die
If I ain't dead already
Ooh girl you know the reason why

In the morning wanna die
In the evening wanna die
If I ain't dead already
Ooh girl you know the reason why

My mother was of the sky
My father was of the earth
But I am of the universe
And you know what it's worth
I'm lonely wanna die
If I ain't dead already
Ooh girl you know the reason why

Y É R   B L U É S
                         1 9 6 8

The eagle picks my eye
The worm he licks my bone
I feel so suicidal
Just like Dylan's Mr. Jones
Lonely wanna die
If I ain't dead already
Ooh girl you know the reason why

Black cloud crossed my mind
Blue mist round my soul
Feel so suicidal
Even hate my rock 'n' roll
Wanna die yeah wanna die
If I ain't dead already
Ooh girl you know the reason why

Yes I'm lonely wanna die
Yes I'm lonely wanna die
If I ain't dead already
Ooh, girl you know the reason why

Yes I'm lonely wanna die
Yes I'm lonely wanna die

MOTHER NATURE'S SON

1968

Born a poor young country boy
Mother Nature's son
All day long I'm sitting singing songs for everyone

Sit beside a mountain stream
See her waters rise
Listen to the pretty sound of music as she flies

Doo doo doo doo doo doo doo doo doo doo doo
Doo doo doo doo doo doo doo doo doo
Doo doo doo

Find me in my field of grass
Mother Nature's son
Swaying daisies sing a lazy song beneath the sun

Doo doo doo doo doo doo doo doo doo doo doo
Doo doo doo doo doo doo doo doo doo
Doo doo doo doo doo doo
Yeah yeah yeah

Mm mm mm mm mm mm mm
Mm mm mm, ooh ooh ooh
Mm mm mm mm mm mm mm
Mm mm mm mm, wah wah wah

Wah, Mother Nature's son

Sexy Sadie

1968

Sexy Sadie what have you done
You made a fool of everyone
You made a fool of everyone
Sexy Sadie ooh what have you done

Sexy Sadie you broke the rules
You layed it down for all to see
You layed it down for all to see
Sexy Sadie oooh you broke the rules

One sunny day the world was waiting for a lover
She came along to turn on everyone
Sexy Sadie (Sexy Sadie) the greatest (She's the greatest) of them all

Sexy Sadie how did you know
The world was waiting just for you
The world was waiting just for you
Sexy Sadie oooh how did you know

Sexy Sadie you'll get yours yet
However big you think you are
However big you think you are
Sexy Sadie oooh you'll get yours yet

We gave her everything we owned just to sit at her table
Just a smile would lighten everything
Sexy Sadie she's the latest and the greatest of them all

She made a fool of everyone
Sexy Sadie

However big you think you are
Sexy Sadie

EVERYBODY'S GOT SOMETHING TO HIDE EXCEPT ME AND MY MONKEY

1968

Come on come on
Come on come on
Come on is such a joy
Come on is such a joy
Come on let's take it easy
Come on let's take it easy
Take it easy take it easy
Everybody's got something to hide 'cept for me and my monkey

(Ooh) The deeper you go the higher you fly
The higher you fly the deeper you go
So come on (Come on) come on
Come on is such a joy
Come on is such a joy
Come on let's make it easy
Come on let's make it easy (Oh)
Take it easy (Yeh yeh yeh) take it easy (Hoo)
Everybody's got something to hide 'cept for me and my monkey

Oh!

Your inside is out and your outside is in
Your outside is in and your inside is out
So come on (Ho) come on (Ho)
Come on is such a joy
Come on is such a joy
Come on let's make it easy
Come on let's make it easy
Make it easy (Hoo) make it easy (Hoo)
Everybody's got something to hide 'cept for me and my monkey

Hey!

Come on, come on, come on, come on, come on
Come on, come on, come on…
Come on, come on, come on, come on, come on
Come on, come on, come on…

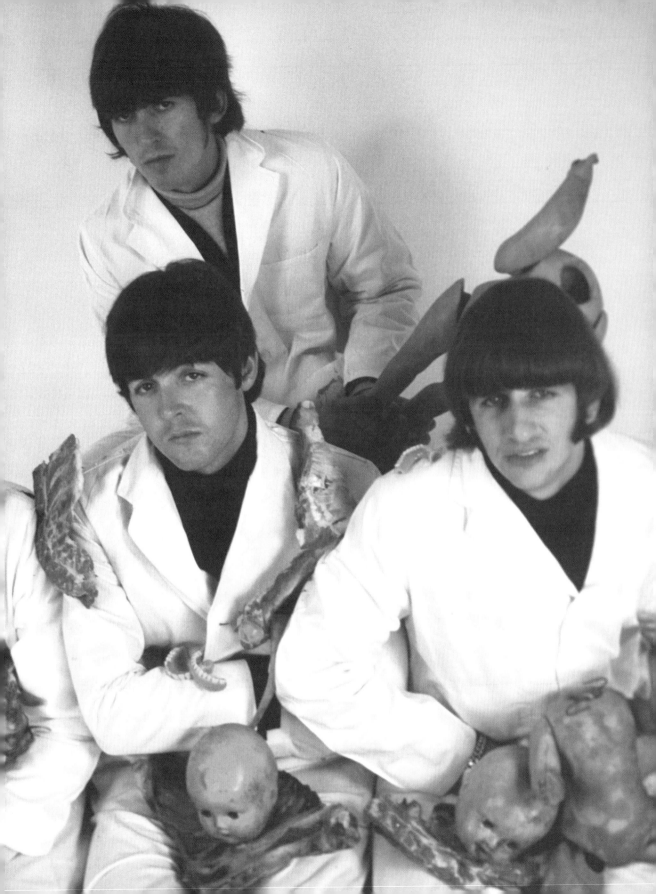

HELTER SKELTER
1968

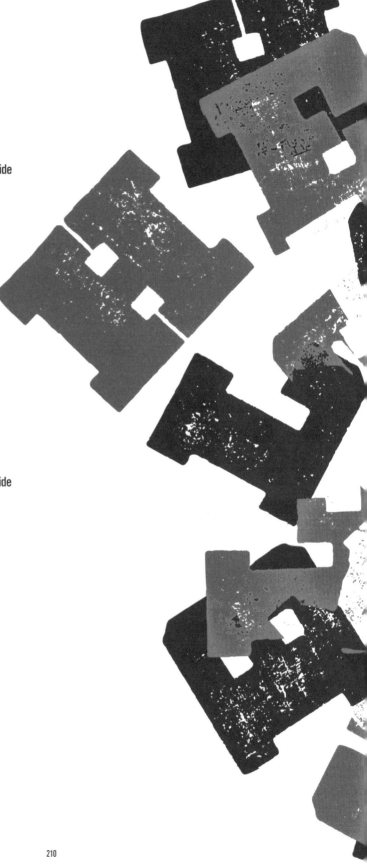

When I get to the bottom I go back to the top of the slide
Where I stop and I turn and I go for a ride
Till I get to the bottom and I see you again
Yeah yeah yeah hey

Do you, don't you want me to love you
I'm coming down fast but I'm miles above you
Tell me tell me tell me come on tell me the answer
Well you may be a lover but you ain't no dancer

Now helter skelter helter skelter
Helter skelter yeah ooh!

Will you, won't you want me to make you
I'm coming down fast but don't let me break you
Tell me tell me tell me the answer
You may be a lover but you ain't no dancer

Look out helter skelter helter skelter
Helter skelter ooh

Look out, cause here she comes

When I get to the bottom I go back to the top of the slide
And I stop and I turn and I go for a ride
And I get to the bottom and I see you again
Yeah yeah yeah

Well do you, don't you want me to make you
I'm coming down fast but don't let me break you
Tell me tell me tell me the answer
You may be a lover but you ain't no dancer

Look out helter skelter helter skelter
Helter skelter

Look out helter skelter
She's coming down fast
Yes she is
Yes she is coming down fast

[Hold the helter skelter, ooh…
Ha ha ha, ha ha ha, alright!
I got blisters on my fingers!]

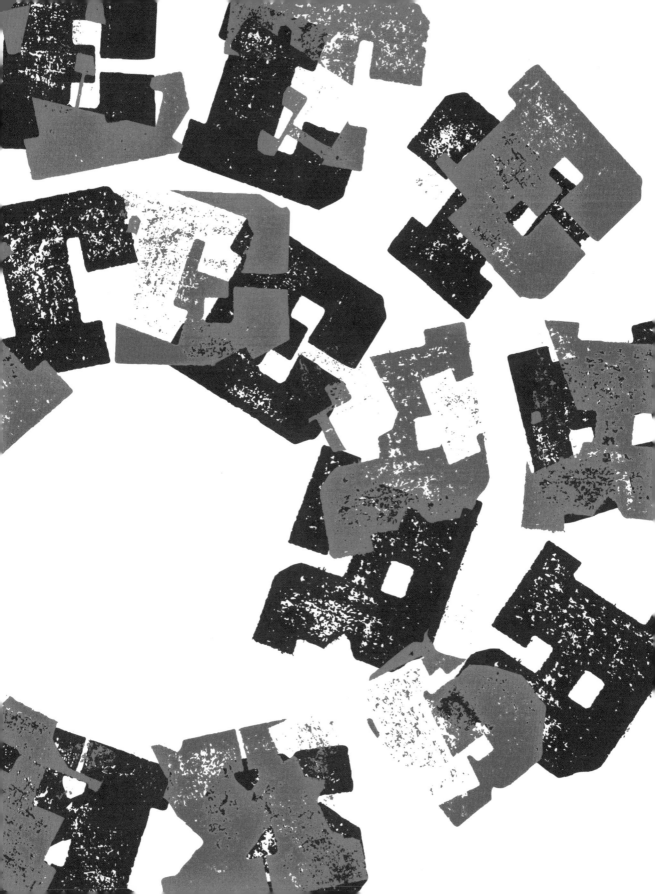

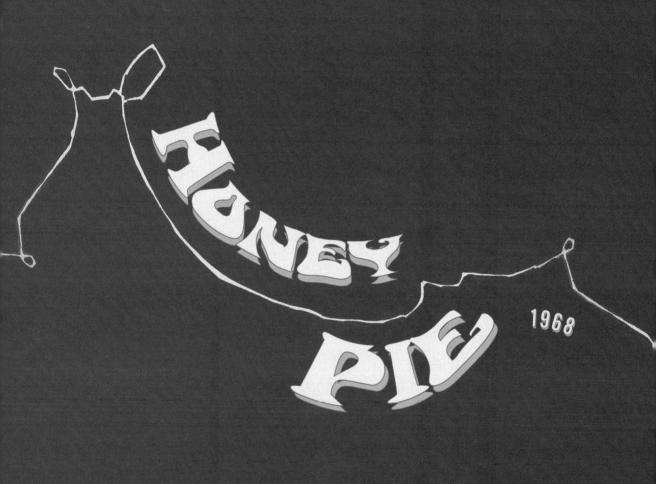

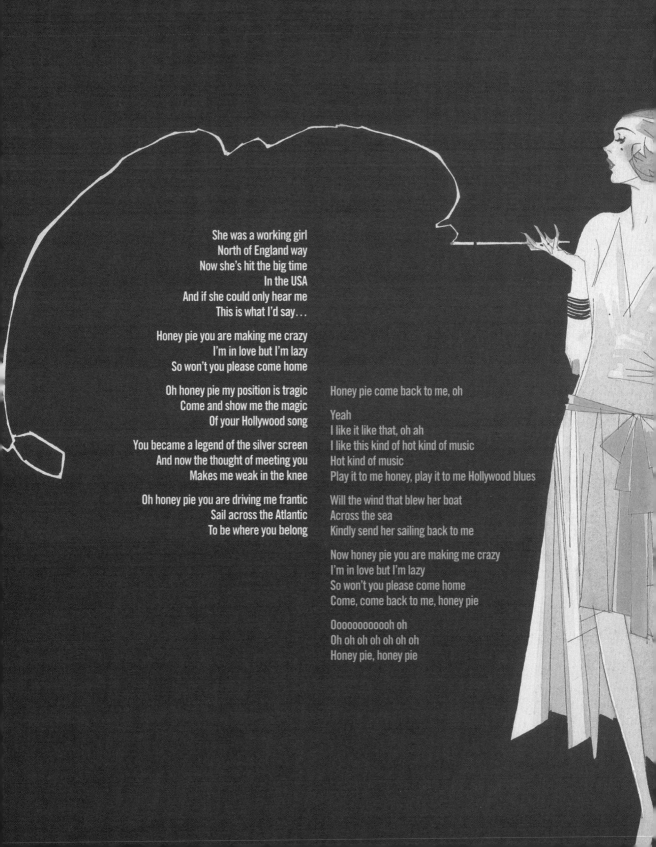

She was a working girl
North of England way
Now she's hit the big time
In the USA
And if she could only hear me
This is what I'd say…

Honey pie you are making me crazy
I'm in love but I'm lazy
So won't you please come home

Oh honey pie my position is tragic
Come and show me the magic
Of your Hollywood song

You became a legend of the silver screen
And now the thought of meeting you
Makes me weak in the knee

Oh honey pie you are driving me frantic
Sail across the Atlantic
To be where you belong

Honey pie come back to me, oh

Yeah
I like it like that, oh ah
I like this kind of hot kind of music
Hot kind of music
Play it to me honey, play it to me Hollywood blues

Will the wind that blew her boat
Across the sea
Kindly send her sailing back to me

Now honey pie you are making me crazy
I'm in love but I'm lazy
So won't you please come home
Come, come back to me, honey pie

Ooooooooooooh oh
Oh oh oh oh oh oh oh
Honey pie, honey pie

REVOL
UTION

Right. Take 2
OK!

You say you want a revolution
Well you know
We all want to change the world
You tell me that it's evolution
Well you know
We all want to change the world
But when you talk about destruction
Don't you know that you can count me out

Don't you know it's gonna be (shooby doo wah) alright (shooby doo wah)
Don't you know it's gonna be (shooby doo wah) alright (shooby doo wah)
Don't you know it's gonna be (shooby doo wah) alright (shooby doo wah)

You say you got a real solution
Well you know
We'd all love to see the plan
You ask me for a contribution
Well you know
We're all doing what we can
But if you want money for people with minds that hate
All I can tell you is brother you have to wait

Don't you know it's gonna be (shooby doo wah) alright (shooby doo wah)
Don't you know it's gonna be (shooby doo wah) alright (shooby doo wah)
Don't you know it's gonna be (shooby doo wah) alright (shooby doo wah)

You say you'll change the constitution
Well you know
We'd all love to change your head
You tell me it's the institution
Well you know
You'd better free your mind instead
But if you go carrying pictures of Chairman Mao
You ain't going to make it with anyone anyhow

Don't you know it's gonna be (shooby doo wah) alright (shooby doo wah)
Don't you know it's gonna be (shooby doo wah) alright (shooby doo wah)
Don't you know it's gonna be (shooby doo wah) alright (shooby doo wah)

Oh, oh, oh, oh, oh, oh, oh, oh, oh, oh, oh
Alright, alright, alright, alright, alright
Alright, alright, alright, alright, alright
Oh,oh,oh,oh,oh,oh
Alright, alright, alright
Alright
Alright

GOOD
NIGHT

1968

Now it's time to say good night
Good night, sleep tight
Now the sun turns out his light
Good night, sleep tight
Dream sweet dreams for me
(Dream sweet)
Dream sweet dreams for you

Close your eyes and I'll close mine
Good night, sleep tight
Now the moon begins to shine
Good night, sleep tight
Dream sweet dreams for me
(Dream sweet)
Dream sweet dreams for you

Mmmmmm
Mmmmmm
Mmmmmmmmmm

Close your eyes and I'll close mine
Good night, sleep tight
Now the sun turns out his light
Good night, sleep tight
Dream sweet dreams for me
(Dream sweet)
Dream sweet dreams for you

Good night everybody
Everybody everywhere
Good night

REVOLUTION

1968

[Bottle of Claret for you if I had realised

Well, do it next time.

I forgot about it, George, I'm sorry. Will you forgive me?

Yes]

Number 9, number 9, number 9,
number 9, number 9, number 9,
number 9, number 9, number 9,
number 9, number 9, number 9,
number 9, number 9, number

Then there's this Welsh Rarebit wearing some brown underpants
About the shortage of grain in Hertfordshire
Everyone of them knew that as time went by they'd get a little
bit older and a little bit slower but it's all the same thing, in this
case manufactured by someone who's always
Umpteen your father's giving it diddly-i-dee
District was leaving, intending to pay for

Number 9, number 9

Who's to know?
Who wants to know?

Number 9, number 9, number 9, number 9,
number 9, number 9, number 9

I sustained nothing worse than
Also for example
Whatever you're doing
A business deal falls through
I informed him on the third night but fortunately

Number 9, number 9, number 9

People ride, people ride
Right! Right! Right!
Right! Right!
Right! Right!

9, number 9
I've missed all of that
It makes me a few days late
Compared with, like, wow!
And weird stuff like that
Taking our sides sometimes
Floral bark
Rouge doctors have brought this specimen

I have nobody's daughter, aha

9, number 9

With the situation

They are standing still

The plan, the telegram

Ooh ooh

Number 9, number

Ooh

A man without terrors from beard to
false as the headmaster reported to me
My son he really can try as they do to find function
Tell what he was saying, and his voice was low and his hive high
And his eyes were low

Alright!

219

Number 9, number 9, number 9
number 9, number 9, number 9
number 9, number 9, number 9
number 9, number 9

So the wife called and we better go to see a surgeon
Or whatever to price it yellow underclothes
So, any road, we went to see the dentist instead
Who gave her a pair of teeth which wasn't any good at all
So instead of that, joined the bloody navy and went to sea

In my broken chair, my wings are broken and so is my hair
I'm not in the mood for wearing

Um da
Aaah

How?
Dogs are for dogging, cats are for catting
Birds for birding and fish for fishing
Lems are for lemming, men are for women

Only to find the night-watchman
Unaware of his presence in the building

Onion soup

Number 9, number 9, number 9
number 9, number 9, number 9

Industrial output
Financial imbalance

Thrusting it between his shoulder blades

The Watusi
The twist

Eldorado

Take this brother, may it serve you well

Maybe it's not that, it's
Ahh
Maybe even then exposure is something
– a difficult thing
I'll be alright. I'll be alright

Exposure
It's almost like being naked
I'll be alright. I'll be alright. I'll be alright

If, you become naked

Two of Us

1970

[I Dig A Pygmy by Charles Hawtrey and the Deaf Aids.
Phase one, in which Doris gets her oats]

Two of us riding nowhere
Spending someone's
Hard earned pay
You and me Sunday driving
Not arriving
On our way back home
We're on our way home
We're on our way home
We're going home

Two of us sending postcards
Writing letters
On my wall
You and me burning matches
Lifting latches
On our way back home
We're on our way home
We're on our way home
We're going home

You and I have memories
Longer than the road that stretches out ahead

Two of us wearing raincoats
Standing so low
In the sun
You and me chasing paper
Getting nowhere
On our way back home
We're on our way home
We're on our way home
We're going home

You and I have memories
Longer than the road that stretches out ahead

Two of us wearing raincoats
Standing solo
In the sun
You and me chasing paper
Getting nowhere
On our way back home
We're on our way home
We're on our way home
We're going home

[We're going home, you better believe it. Goodbye]

CRY BABY CRY 1968

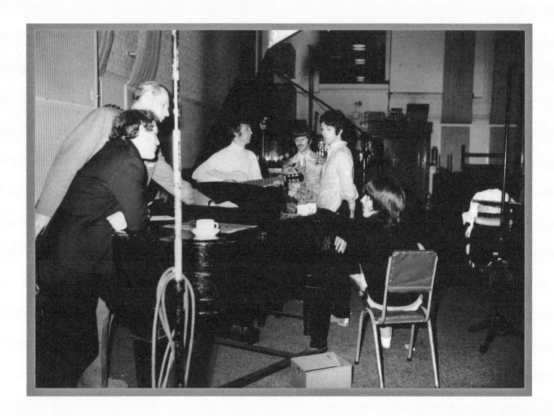

Cry baby cry, make your mother sigh
She's old enough to know better
The King of Marigold was in the kitchen
Cooking breakfast for the queen
The queen was in the parlour
Playing piano for the children of the king
Cry baby cry, make your mother sigh
She's old enough to know better
So cry baby cry

The king was in the garden
Picking flowers for a friend who came to play
The queen was in the playroom
Painting pictures for the children's holiday
Cry baby cry, make your mother sigh
She's old enough to know better
So cry baby cry

The Duchess of Kirkaldy always smiling
And arriving late for tea
The duke was having problems
With a message at the local bird and bee
Cry baby cry, make your mother sigh
She's old enough to know better
So cry baby cry
At twelve o'clock a meeting round the table
For a seance in the dark
With voices out of nowhere
Put on specially by the children for a lark
Cry baby cry, make your mother sigh
She's old enough to know better
So cry baby cry cry cry
Cry baby, make your mother sigh
She's old enough to know better
Cry baby cry
Cry cry cry, make your mother sigh
She's old enough to know better
So cry baby cry

Can you take me back where I came
from, can you take me back?
Can you take me back where I came
from, brother can you take me back
Can you take me back home?
Can you take me back where I came
from, can you take me back?

DIG A PONY

I dig a pony
Well you can celebrate anything you want
Yes you can celebrate anything you want
Oh!
I do a road hog
Well you can penetrate any place you go
Yes you can penetrate any place you go I told you so
All I want is you
Everything has got to be just like you want it to because
I pick a moon dog
Well you can radiate everything you are
Yes you can radiate everything you are
Oh now
I roll a stoney
Well you can imitate everyone you know
Yes you can imitate everyone you know I told you so
All I want is you
Everything has got to be just like you want it to
Because…

Ooh now
I feel the wind blow
Well you can indicate everything you see
Yes you can indicate anything you see
Oh now
I, load a lorry
Well you can syndicate any boat you row
Yeah you can syndicate any boat you row
I told you so,
All I want is you
Everything has got to be just like you want it to
Because…

across the

1970

Words are flowing out like endless rain into a paper cup
They slither wildly as they slip away across the universe
Pools of sorrow, waves of joy are drifting through my opened mind
Possessing and caressing me
Jai Guru Deva OM

Nothing's gonna change my world
Nothing's gonna change my world
Nothing's gonna change my world
Nothing's gonna change my world

Images of broken light which dance before me like a million eyes
They call me on and on across the universe
Thoughts meander like a restless wind inside a letter box
They tumble blindly as they make their way across the universe
Jai Guru Deva OM

Nothing's gonna change my world
Nothing's gonna change my world
Nothing's gonna change my world
Nothing's gonna change my world

Sounds of laughter, shades of life are ringing through my opened ears
Inciting and inviting me
Limitless undying love which shines around me like a million suns
And calls me on and on, across the universe
Jai Guru Deva OM

Nothing's gonna change my world
Nothing's gonna change my world
Nothing's gonna change my world
Nothing's gonna change my world

Jai Guru Deva
Jai Guru Deva
Jai Guru Deva
Jai Guru Deva
Jai Guru Deva

universe

an intimate bioscopic experience with

THE BEATLES

APPLE

An **abkco** managed company

presents

"Let it be"

Produced by NEIL ASPINALL   Directed by MICHAEL LINDSAY-HOGG

TECHNICOLOR®

G ALL AGES ADMITTED General Audiences

United Artists
Entertainment from
Transamerica Corporation

LET IT BE

ORIGINAL MOTION PICTURE SCORE
AVAILABLE ON APPLE RECORDS

When I find myself in times of trouble
Mother Mary comes to me
Speaking words of wisdom, let it be
And in my hour of darkness
She is standing right in front of me
Speaking words of wisdom, let it be
Let it be, let it be
Let it be, let it be
Whisper words of wisdom, let it be

And when the broken-hearted people
Living in the world agree
There will be an answer, let it be
For though they may be parted
There is still a chance that they will see
There will be an answer, let it be
Let it be, let it be
Let it be, let it be
Yeah, there will be an answer, let it be

Let it be, let it be
Let it be, let it be
Whisper words of wisdom, let it be

Let it be, let it be
Ah, let it be, yeah, let it be
Whisper words of wisdom, let it be

And when the night is cloudy
There is still a light that shines on me
Shine until tomorrow, let it be
I wake up to the sound of music
Mother Mary comes to me
Speaking words of wisdom, let it be
Let it be, let it be
Let it be, yeah, let it be
Oh, there will be an answer, let it be
Let it be, let it be
Let it be, yeah, let it be
There will be an answer, let it be
Let it be, let it be,
Let it be, yeah, let it be
Whisper words of wisdom, let it be

"Let it be"

1970

I've got a feeling

I've got a feeling, a feeling deep inside
Oh yeah, oh yeah, that's right
I've got a feeling, a feeling I can't hide
Oh no no, oh no, oh no
Yeah yeah I've got a feeling yeah

Oh please believe me
I'd hate to miss the train
Oh yeah, yeah, oh yeah
And if you leave me
I won't be late again
Oh no, oh no, oh no
Yeah yeah I've got a feeling yeah
I've got a feeling

All these years I've been wandering around
Wondering how come nobody told me
All that I was looking for was somebody
Who looked like you

I've got a feeling, that keeps me on my toes
Oh yeah, oh yeah
I've got a feeling, I think that everybody knows
Oh yeah, oh yeah, oh yeah
Yeah yeah I've got a feeling yeah
Yeah

Everybody had a hard year
Everybody had a good time
Everybody had a wet dream
Everybody saw the sunshine
Oh yeah, (oh yeah) oh yeah, oh yeah

Everybody had a good year
Everybody let their hair down
Everybody pulled their socks up
Everybody put their foot down
Oh yeah

Everybody had a good year
(I got a feeling)
Everybody had a hard time
(A feeling deep inside, oh yeah)
Everybody had a wet dream
(Oh yeah)
Everybody saw the sunshine
(I've got a feeling)
Everybody had a good year
(A feeling I can't hide)
Everybody let their hair down
(Oh no)
Everybody pulled their socks up
(Oh, no no no)
Everybody put their foot down
Oh yeah.
I've got a feeling
I've got a feeling
I've got a feeling

[Oh, my soul! It's so hard]

THE LONG AND WINDING ROAD

1970

The long and winding road
That leads to your door
Will never disappear
I've seen that road before
It always leads me here
Lead me to your door

The wild and windy night that the rain washed away
Has left a pool of tears crying for the day
Why leave me standing here
Let me know the way

Many times I've been alone and many times I've cried
Anyway you'll never know the many ways I've tried
And still they lead me back to the long winding road
You left me standing here a long, long time ago
Don't leave me waiting here, lead me to you door

But still they lead me back
To the long winding road
You left me standing here
A long, long time ago
Don't keep me waiting here
Lead me to you door
Yeah, yeah, yeah, yeah

ONE AFTER 909 1970

My baby says she's trav'ling on the one after 909
I said move over honey I'm travelling on that line
I said move over once, move over twice
Come on baby don't be cold as ice
She said she's trav'ling on the one after 909

I begged her not to go and I begged her on my bended knees
You're only fooling around, only fooling around with me
She said move over once, move over twice
Come on baby don't be cold as ice
She said I'm trav'ling on the one after 909

Pick up my bag, run to the station
Railman says you've got the the wrong location
Pick up the bag, run right home
Then I find I got the number wrong

She said she's trav'ling on the one after 909
I said move over honey I'm travelling on that line
I said move over once, move over twice
Come on baby don't be cold as ice
She said she's trav'ling on the one after 909

Pick up my bag, run to the station
Railman says you've got the wrong location
Well, pick up my bag, run right home
Then I find I got the number wrong

She said she's trav'ling on the one after 909
I said move over honey I'm travelling on that line
I said move over once, move over twice
Come on baby don't be cold as ice
I said we're trav'ling on the one after 90
 said we're trav'ling on the one after 90
I said we're trav'ling on the one after 909

[Oh Danny Boy, the old summer is calling]

GET BACK
1969

Jojo was a man who thought he was a loner
But he knew it wouldn't last
Jojo left his home in Tucson, Arizona
For some California grass
Get back, get back
Get back to where you once belonged
Get back, get back
Get back to where you once belonged
Get back Jojo
Go home
Get back, get back
Get back to where you once belonged
Get back, get back
Get back to where you once belonged
Get back Jo

Sweet Loretta Martin thought she was a woman
But she was another man
All the girls around her say she's got it coming
But she gets it while she can
Oh get back, get back
Get back to where you once belonged
Get back, get back
Get back to where you once belonged
Get back Loretta
Go home
Oh get back, yeah get back
Get back to where you once belonged
Get back, get back
Get back to where you once belonged

Ooh, oh, oh,
Get back Loretta
Your mama's waiting for you
Wearing her high-heel shoes
And a low-neck sweater
Get back home Loretta
Get back
Oh, get back
Get back to where you once belonged
Oh, get back
Get back, get back, oh yeah
Jojo, oh yeah

[I'd like to thank you on behalf of the group
  and ourselves and I hope we've passed the
  audition]

DON'T LET ME DOWN

1970

Don't let me down, don't let me down
Don't let me down, don't let me down

Nobody ever loved me like she does
Ooh, she does, yeah, she does
And if somebody loved me like she do me
Ooh, she do me, yes, she does

Don't let me down, don't let me down
Don't let me down, don't let me down

I'm in love for the first time
Don't you know it's gonna last
It's a love that lasts forever
It's a love that has no past

Don't let me down, don't let me down
Don't let me down, don't let me down

And from the first time that she really done me
Ooh, she done me, she done me good
I guess nobody ever really done me
Ooh, she done me, she done me good

Don't let me down,
Hey don't let me down
Heeeee, don't let me down

Don't let me down
Don't let me down
Don't let me let down
Can you dig it? Don't let me down

THE BALLAD OF JOHN AND YOKO

1969

Standing in the dock at Southampton
Trying to get to Holland or France
The man in the mac said
"You've got to go back"
You know they didn't even give us a chance
Christ you know it ain't easy
You know how hard it can be
The way things are going
They're gonna crucify me

Finally made the plane into Paris
Honeymooning down by the Seine
Peter Brown called to say
"You can make it OK
You can get married in Gibraltar, near Spain"
Christ you know it ain't easy
You know how hard it can be
The way things are going
They're gonna crucify me

Drove from Paris to the Amsterdam Hilton
Talking in our beds for a week
The newspeople said
"Say what you doing in bed?"
I said, "We're only trying to get us some peace"
Christ you know it ain't easy
You know how hard it can be
The way things are going
They're gonna crucify me

Saving up your money for a rainy day
Giving all your clothes to charity
Last night the wife said
"Oh boy, when you're dead
You don't take nothing with you
But your soul. Think!"

Made a lightning trip to Vienna
Eating chocolate cake in a bag
The newspapers said
"She's gone to his head
They look just like two gurus in drag"
Christ you know it ain't easy
You know how hard it can be
The way things are going
They're gonna crucify me

Caught the early plane back to London
Fifty acorns tied in a sack
The men from the press said
"We wish you success
It's good to have the both of you back"
Christ you know it ain't easy
You know how hard it can be
The way things are going
They're gonna crucify me
The way things are going
They're gonna crucify me

You know my

1970

You know my name, look up the number
You know my name, look up the number
You you know you know my name
You you know you know my name

Good evening and welcome to Slaggers
Featuring Denis O'Bell
Come on Ringo, let's hear it for Denis

Good evening, you know my name
Well then look up my number
You know my name
That's right, look up my number
You you know you know my name
You you know you know my name
You know my name
Ba ba ba ba ba ba ba ba

Look up the number
You know my name
That's right, look up the number
Oh you know you know
You know my name
You know you know
You know my name
Huh huh huh huh, you know my name
Ba ba ba bum, look up the number
You know my name, look up the number
You-a you know you know my name
Baby you-a you know you know my name
You know you know my name
You know you know my name

Let's hear it. Go on Denis let's hear it for
Denis O'Bell

You know my name
You know you know my name
You know you know my name
Prrr you know my name and the number
You know my name and the number
You know you know my name
Look up me number
You know my name
You know my number too
You know my number three
You know my number four
Oh you know my name
You know my number too
You know my name you know my number
What's up with you?
You know my name
That's right?
Yeah

name

Paul McCartney

Ringo Starr

George Harrison

John Lennon

1969

Shoot me. Shoot me. Shoot me. Shoot me.

Here come old flat top,
He come grooving up slowly
He got juju eyeball, he want holy roller
He got hair down to his knee
Got to be a joker he just do what he please

Shoot me. Shoot me. Shoot me. Shoot me.

He wear no shoeshine,
He got toe-jam football
He got monkey finger,
He shoot coca-cola
He say "I know you, you know me"
One thing I can tell you is you've got to be free
Come together right now over me

Shoot me. Shoot me. Shoot me.

He bag production,
He got walrus gumboot
He got Ono sideboard
He want spinal cracker
He got feet down below his knee
Hold you in his arms, yeah you can feel his disease
Come together right now over me

(Right!
Come, oh, come, come, come)

He roller-coaster,
He got early warning
He got muddy water,
He want mojo filter
He say "One and one and one is three"
Got to be good-looking cause he's so hard to see
Come together right now over me

Shoot me. Shoot me. Shoot me

Oh,
Come together, yeah
Come together, yeah
Come together, yeah
Come together, yeah
Come together, yeah
Come together, yeah
Come together, yeah
Ah. Come together, yeah
Come together, yeah

OH! DARLING

1969

Oh! Darling, please believe me
I'll never do you no harm
Believe me when I tell you
I'll never do you no harm

Oh! Darling, if you leave me
I'll never make it alone
Believe me when I thank you, ooo
Don't ever leave me alone

When you told me
You didn't need me anymore
Well you know I nearly broke down and cried
When you told me
You didn't need me anymore
Well you know I nearly broke down and died

Oh! Darling, if you leave me
I'll never make it alone
Believe me when I tell you
I'll never do you no harm
Believe me darling

When you told me
You didn't need me anymore
Well you know I nearly broke down and cried
When you told me
You didn't need me anymore
Well you know I nearly broke down and died

Oh! Darling, please believe me
I'll never let you down
Oh, believe me darling
Believe me when I tell you, ooo
I'll never do you no harm

Joan was quizzical, studied pataphysical science in the home
Late nights all alone with a test-tube
Ohh oh oh oh
Maxwell Edison majoring in medicine
Calls her on the phone
"Can I take you out to the pictures, Joan?"
But as she's getting ready to go
A knock comes on the door

Bang, bang, Maxwell's silver hammer came down upon her head
Bang, bang, Maxwell's silver hammer made sure that she was dead

Back in school again Maxwell plays the fool again
Teacher gets annoyed
Wishing to avoid an unpleasant scene
She tells Max to stay when the class has gone away
So he waits behind
Writing 50 times "I must not be so" Oh oh oh
But when she turns her back on the boy
He creeps up from behind

Bang, bang, Maxwell's silver hammer came down upon her head
Do do do do do
Bang, bang, Maxwell's silver hammer made sure that she was dead

P.C. 31 said "We caught a dirty one"
Maxwell stands alone
Painting testimonial pictures
Ohh oh oh oh
Rose and Valerie screaming from the gallery
Say he must go free (Maxwell must go free)
The judge does not agree and he tells them so oh oh oh
But as the words are leaving his lips
A noise comes from behind

Bang, bang, Maxwell's silver hammer came down upon his head
Do do do do do
Bang, Bang, Maxwell's silver hammer made sure that he was dead
Wow wow wow oh!
Do do do do do
Silver hammer Man

I WANT YOU (SHE'S SO HEAVY)

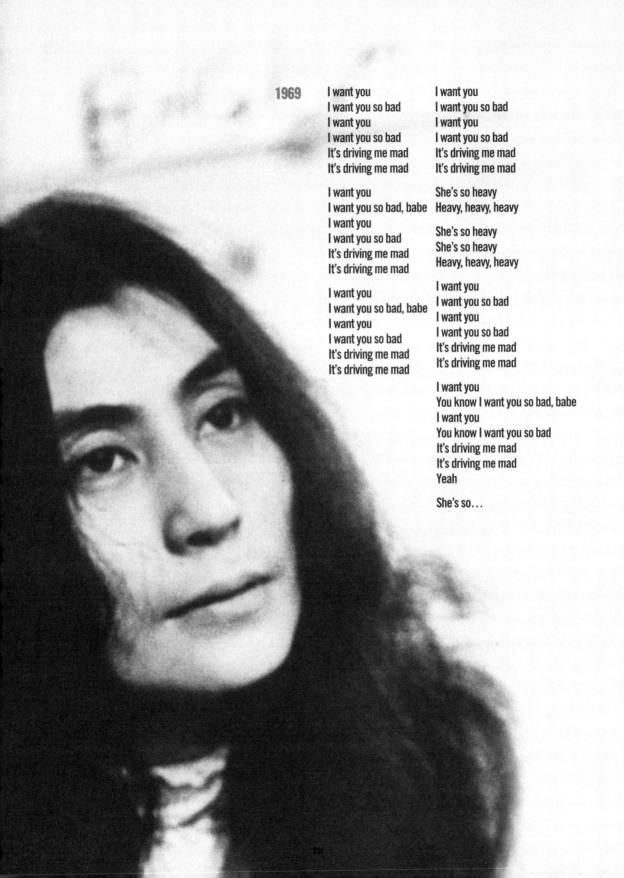

1969

I want you
I want you so bad
I want you
I want you so bad
It's driving me mad
It's driving me mad

I want you
I want you so bad, babe
I want you
I want you so bad
It's driving me mad
It's driving me mad

I want you
I want you so bad, babe
I want you
I want you so bad
It's driving me mad
It's driving me mad

I want you
I want you so bad
I want you
I want you so bad
It's driving me mad
It's driving me mad

She's so heavy
Heavy, heavy, heavy

She's so heavy
She's so heavy
Heavy, heavy, heavy

I want you
I want you so bad
I want you
I want you so bad
It's driving me mad
It's driving me mad

I want you
You know I want you so bad, babe
I want you
You know I want you so bad
It's driving me mad
It's driving me mad
Yeah

She's so...

1969

Aaaaaahhhhhh...
Because the world is round
It turns me on
Because the world is round...
aaaaaahhhhhh

Because the wind is high
It blows my mind
Because the wind is high... aaaaaaaahhhh

BECAUSE

Love is old, love is new
Love is all, love is you

Because the sky is blue
It makes me cry
Because the sky is blue... aaaaaaaahhhh

Aaaaahhhhhhhhhh...
Aaaaahhhhhhhhhh...
Aaaaahhhhhhhhhh...

YOU NEVER GIVE ME YOUR MONEY

You never give me your money
You only give me your funny paper
And in the middle of negotiations
You break down

I never give you my number
I only give you my situation
And in the middle of investigation
I breakdown

Out of college, money spent
See no future, pay no rent
All the money's gone, nowhere to go
Any job got the sack
Monday morning, turning back
Yellow lorry slow, nowhere to go
But oh, that magic feeling, nowhere to go
Oh, that magic feeling, nowhere to go
Nowhere to go

Aaaaahhhhhhhhhh…
Aaaaahhhhhhhhhh…
Aaaaahhhhhhhhhh…

One sweet dream
Pick up the bags and get in the limousine
Soon we'll be away from here
Step on the gas and wipe that tear away
One sweet dream came true today
Came true today
Came true today (Yes it did)

One two three four five six seven
All good children go to Heaven
One two three four five six seven
All good children go to Heaven
One two three four five six seven
All good children go to Heaven
One two three four five six seven
All good children go to Heaven
One two three four five six seven
All good children go to Heaven
One two three four five six seven
All good children go to Heaven
One two three four five six seven
All good children go to Heaven
One two three four five six seven
All good children go to Heaven

THIS NOTE IS LEGAL TENDER
FOR ALL DEBTS, PUBLIC AND PRIVATE

Anna Escobedo Cabral

Treasurer of the United States.

C 3

SERIES
1969
A

100

1969

Aaaaahhhhhhhhhh…
Here comes the sun king
Here comes the sun king
Everybody's laughing
Everybody's happy
Here comes the sun king

Cuando para mucho mi amore
de felice corazòn
Mondo paparazzi mi amore chica
verde parasol
Questo obrigado tanta mucho
que can eat it carousel

BAGISM

48

POLYTHENE PAM

1969

Well you should see Polythene Pam
She's so good-looking but she looks like a man
Well you should see her in drag dressed in her polythene bag
Yes you should see Polythene Pam
Yeah yeah yeah

Get a dose of her in jackboots and kilt
She's killer-diller when she's dressed to the hilt
She's the kind of a girl that makes the "News of the World"
Yes you could say she was attractively built

Yeah yeah yeah

49

MEAN MR. MUSTARD

1969

Mean Mister Mustard sleeps in the park
Shaves in the dark trying to save paper
Sleeps in a hole in the road
Saving up to buy some clothes
Keeps a ten-bob note up his nose
Such a mean old man
Such a mean old man

His sister Pam works in a shop
She never stops, she's a go-getter
Takes him out to look at the queen
Only place that he's ever been
Always shouts out something obscene
Such a dirty old man
Dirty old man

SHE CAME IN THROUGH THE BATHROOM WINDOW

1969

(Oh, listen to that mouth,
ha ha ha ha, wow look out)

She came in through the bathroom window
Protected by a silver spoon
But now she sucks her thumb and wanders
By the banks of her own lagoon

Didn't anybody tell her?
Didn't anybody see?
Sunday's on the phone to Monday
Tuesday's on the phone to me

She said she'd always been a dancer
She worked at 15 clubs a day
And though she thought I knew the answer
Well I knew but I could not say

And so I quit the police department
And got myself a steady job
And though she tried her best to help me
She could steal but she could not rob

Didn't anybody tell her?
Didn't anybody see?
Sunday's on the phone to Monday
Tuesday's on the phone to me
Oh yeah

HER MAJESTY

1 9 6 9

Her majesty's a pretty nice girl
But she doesn't have a lot to say
Her majesty's a pretty nice girl
But she changes from day to day
I wanna tell her that I love her a lot
But I gotta get a belly full of wine
Her majesty's a pretty nice girl
Some day I'm gonna make her mine
Some day I'm gonna make her mine

GOLDEN
GOLDEN
GOLDEN

1969

Once there was a way to get back homeward
Once there was a way to get back home
Sleep pretty darling do not cry
And I will sing a lullabye

Golden slumbers fill your eyes
Smiles awake you when you rise
Sleep pretty darling do not cry
And I will sing a lullabye

Once there was a way to get back homeward
Once there was a way to get back home
Sleep pretty darling do not cry
And I will sing a lullabye

SLUMBERS
SLUMBERS
SLUMBERS

```
Eastman and Eastman
39 West 54th Street
New York
New York 10019                          18th April 1969


Attention Lee Eastman, Esq.

Dear Mr. Eastman,

     This is to inform you of the fact that you are not
authorized to act or to hold yourself out as the attourney
or legal representative of "The Beatles" or of any of the
companies which the Beatles own or control.

     We recognize that you are authorized to act for
Paul McCartney, personally, and in this regard we will
instruct our representatives to give you the fullest co-
operation.

     We would appreciate your forwarding to

          ABKCO Industries Inc.
          1700 Broadway
          New York
          N.Y.

all documents, correspondence and files which you hold
in your possession relating to the affairs of the Beatles,
or any of the companies which the Beatles own or control.

                    Very truly yours,


          John Lennon         John Lennon


          Richard Starkey     R Starkey


          George Harrison     George Harrison
```

Carry That Weight
1 9 6 9

Boy, you're gonna carry that weight
Carry that weight a long time
Boy, you're gonna carry that weight
Carry that weight a long time

Boy, you're gonna carry that weight
Carry that weight a long time
Boy, you're gonna carry that weight
Carry that weight a long time

I never give you my pillow
I only send you my invitations
And in the middle of the celebrations
I break down

PAUL QUITS THE BEATLES

nd

axi

McCartney . . . . a dea[...]
over policy with John L[...]

By DON SHORT

PAUL McCARTNEY has quit the Beatles. The shock news must mean the end of Britain's most famous pop group, which has been idolised by millions the world over for nearly ten years.

Today 28-year-old McCartney will announce his decision, and the reasons for it, in a no-holds-barred statement.

It follows months of strife over policy in Apple, the Beatles' controlling organisation, and an ever-growing rift between McCartney and his song-writing partner, John Lennon.

McCartney and Lennon are rated one of the greatest popular songwriting teams of the century.

But there is little doubt that McCartney's decision [...] to an end.

'Deeply cut up' after policy row

about it all and his attitudes towards Mr. Klein.

Since the Klein appointment, Paul has refused to go to the Apple offices to work daily.

He kept silent and stayed [at] his St. John's Wood home [...] tographer wife

that hastened Paul's decision to quit. John Lennon, on his marriage to Yoko Ono, set out on projects of his own. Ringo went into films, and George stepped in as a record producer.

Today McCartney will reveal his own plans for a solo programme. [...] include a full-

THE END

1969

Oh yeah, all right
Are you going to be in my dreams
Tonight?

Love you
Love you
Love you
Love you
Love you
Love you
Love you
Love you
Love you
Love you
Love you
Love you

Love you
Love you
Love you
Love you
Love you
Love you
Love you
Love you
Love you
Love you
Love you

And in the end
The love you take
Is equal to the love
You make

I'LL BE ON
MY WAY

1994

The sun is fading away
That's the end of the day
As the June light turns to moonlight
I'll be on my way

Just one kiss and I'll go
Don't hide the tears that don't show
As the June light turns to moonlight
I'll be on my way

To where the winds don't blow
And golden rivers flow
This way will I go

They were right I was wrong
True love didn't last long
As the June light turns to moonlight
I'll be on my way hey

To where the winds don't blow
And golden rivers flow
This way will I go

They were right I was wrong
True love didn't last long
As the June light turns to moonlight
I'll be on my way hey
I'll be on my way oh
I'll be on my way oh
I'll be on my way

Free as

Free as a bird
It's the next best thing to be
Free as a bird

Home, home and dry
Like a homing bird I'll fly
As a bird on wings

Whatever happened to
The lives that we once knew?
Can we really live without each other?

Where did we lose the touch
That seemed to mean so much?
It always made me feel so...

Free as a bird
Like the next best thing to be
Free as a bird

Home, home and dry
Like a homing bird I'll fly
As a bird on wings

Whatever happened to
The life that we once knew?
Always made me feel so free

Ah...
Ah...
Ah...

Free as a bird
It's the next best thing to be
Free as a bird
Free as a bird
Free as a bird
Oooooo

Free...

a Bird 1995

271

All my little plans and schemes
Lost like some forgotten dreams
Seems that all I really was doing
Was waiting for you

Just like little girls and boys
Playing with their little toys
Seems like all they really were doing
Was waiting for love

No need to be alone
No need to be alone
It's real love, it's real
Yes it's real love, it's real

From this moment on I know
Exactly where my life will go
Seems that all I really was doing
Was waiting for love

1996

No need to be afraid
No need to be afraid
It's real love, it's real
Yes it's real love, it's real

Thought I'd been in love before
But in my heart, I wanted more
Seems like all I really was doing
Was waiting for you

No need to be alone
Don't need to be alone

It's real love, it's real
It's real love, it's real
Yes it's real love, it's real
It's real love, it's real
Yes it's real love, it's real
It's real love, it's real
Yes it's real love, it's real
It's real love, it's real

ANOTHER BEATLES CHRISTMAS SHOW

THE BEATLES

CHRISTMAS TIME
(IS HERE AGAIN)

1995

Here's the fan's new remix. Take 444

Christmas time is here again
Christmas time is here again
Christmas time is here again
Christmas time is here again

Ain't been 'round since you know when
Christmas time is here again
O U T spells out

Christmas time is here again
Christmas time is here again
Christmas time is here again
Christmas time is here again

Ain't been 'round since you know when
Christmas time is here again
O U T spells out

Christmas time is here again
Christmas time is here again
Christmas time is here again
Christmas time is here again

Ain't been 'round since you know when
Christmas time is here again
O U T spells out

Christmas time is here again
Christmas time is here again
Christmas time is here again
Christmas time is here again

TIME	TITLE	
	TONES N.R. OUT 1K, 10K, 70Hz, DOLBY TONE 2TRACK **MONO**	
	— SIDE 1 —	
:29	LIKE DREAMERS DO	BSR-1111-A
:17	MONEY	
:19	TAKE GOOD CARE OF MY BABY	
2:17	THREE COOL CATS	
:57	SURE TO FALL — SIDE 2 —	11:39 = TM
'46	LOVE OF THE LOVED	BSR-1111-B
:14	MEMPHIS	
:59	CRYIN' WAITIN' HOPING	
:50	TIL THERE WAS YOU	
:57	SEARCHIN'	

Like Dreamers Do

1995

I, I saw a girl in my dreams
And so it seems that I will love her
Oh you, you are that girl in my dreams
And so it seems that I will love you
And I waited for your kiss
Waited for the bliss
Like dreamers do
And I,
Oh I'll be there, yeah
Waiting for you, you, you, you, you, you

You, you came just one dream ago
And now I know that I will love you
Oh I knew when you first said hello
That's how I know that I will love you
And I waited for your kiss
Waited for the bliss
Like dreamers do
And I
Oh I'll be there, yeah
Waiting for you, you, you, you, you

You, you came just one dream ago
And now I know that I will love you
Oh I knew when you first said hello
That's how I know that I will love you
And I waited for your kiss
Waited for the bliss
Like dreamers do
Oh like dreamers do
Like dreamers do

HELLO LITTLE GIRL

1 9 9 5

Hello little girl
Hello little girl
Hello little girl

When I see you everyday
I say, "Mm mm hello little girl"
When you're passing on your way
I say, "Mm mm hello little girl"
When I see you passing by
I cry, "Mm mm hello little girl"
When I try to catch your eye
I cry, "Mm mm hello little girl"

I send you flowers, but you don't care
You never seem to see me standing there
I often wonder what you're thinking of I hope
it's me and love love love
So I hope there'll come a day
When you'll say, "Mm you're my little girl"

It's not the first time that it's happened to me
It's been a long lonely time
It's so funny, funny to see that I'm
 about to lose my my-my-my-mind

So I hope there'll come a day
When you say, "Mm mm
You're my little girl, mm mm mm
You're my little girl, mm mm mm"
You're my little girl, oh yeah
You're my little girl

Do do do do do

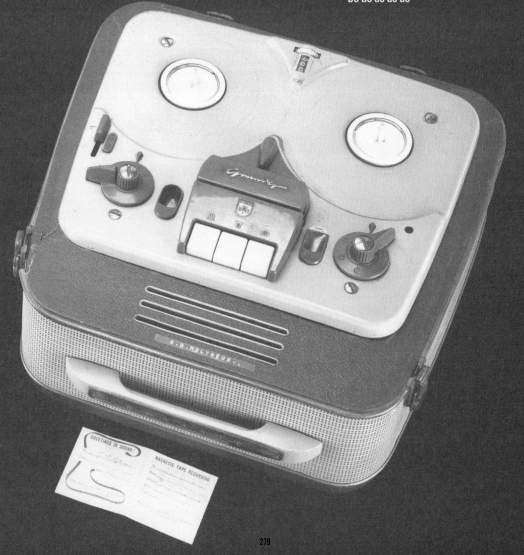

If You've Got Trouble

1996

If you've got trouble
Then you got less trouble than me
You say you're worried
You can't be as worried as me (Oh oh)

You're quite content to be bad
With all the advantage you had over me
Just cause you're trouble
Then don't bring your troubles to me

I don't think it's funny
When you ask for money and things
Especially when you're standing there
Wearing diamonds and rings (Oh oh)

You think I'm soft in the head
Well try someone softer instead anything
It's not so funny
When you know what money can bring

You better leave me alone
I don't need a thing from you
You better take yourself home
Go and count a ring or two

If you've got trouble
Then you got less trouble than me
You say you're worried
You can't be as worried as me

You're quite content to be bad
With all the advantage you had over me
Just cause you're trouble
Then don't bring your troubles to me

(Ah rock on, anybody)

You better leave me alone
I don't need a thing from you
You better take yourself home
Go and count a ring or two

If you've got trouble
Then you got less trouble than me
You say you're worried
You can't be as worried as me (Oh oh)

You're quite contend to be bad
With all the vantage you had over me
Just cause you're trouble
And don't bring your troubles to me
Just cause you're trouble
And don't bring your troubles to me

THAT MEANS A LOT

1 9 9 6

A friend says that your love
Won't mean a lot
But you know that your love
Is all you've got
At times things are so fine
And at times they're not
But when she says she loves you
That means a lot

A friend says that a love
Is never true
But you know that this
Can't apply to you
A touch can mean so much
When it's all you've got
And when she says she loves you
That means a lot

Love can be deep inside
Love can be suicide
Can't you see you can't hide
What you feel when it's real

A friend says that your love
Won't mean a lot
But you know that your love
Is all you've got
A touch can mean so much
When it's all you've got
But when she says she loves you
That means a lot

Can't you see, yeah
Can't you see, yeah
Can't you see, yeah
Can't you see, yeah
Can't you see, yeah
Can't you see, yeah
Can't you see, yeah
Can't you see, yeah

JUNK

1996

Motorcars
Handlebars
Bicycles for two
Broken hearted jubilee

Parachutes
Army boots
Sleeping bags for two
Nah nah nah nah jamboree

Buy buy...

Motorcars
Handlebars
Bicycles for two
Broken hearted jubilee

Parachutes
Army boots
Sleeping bags for you
Nah nah nah jamboree

La la la la la
Why why, says the sign
In the yard

Buy buy, says the sign
In the shop window
Why why, says the junk
In the yard

WHAT'S THE NEW MARY JANE?

1996

She looks as an African Queen
She eating twelve chapatis and cream
She tastes as Mongolian lamb
She coming from out of Bahran
What a shame Mary Jane had a pain at the party
What a shame Mary Jane what a shame
Mary Jane had a pain at the party

She like to be married with Yeti
He grooving such cookie spaghetti
She jumping as Mexican bean
To make that her body morphine
What a shame Mary Jane had a pain at the party
What a shame Mary Jane what a shame
Mary Jane had a pain at the party

She catch Patagonian pancake
With that one and gin party make
She having always good contact
She making with Apple and contract
What a shame Mary Jane had a pain at the party
What a shame Mary Jane what a shame
Mary Jane had a pain at the party

All together now
What a shame Mary Jane had a pain at the party
What a shame what what a shame Mary
Jane had a pain at the party
What a shame what a shame what a shame what a shame
Mary Jane had a pain at the party

What a shame what a shame what a shame what a shame
Mary Jane had a pain at the party
What a shame what a shame
Mary Jane had a pain at the party
What a shame what a shame what a shame
Mary Jane had a pain at the party
What a shame Mary Jane Mary Jane had a pain at the party
What a shame Mary Jane what a shame
Mary Jane had a pain at the party
What a shame Mary Jane what a shame

She looks as an African Queen
She tastes as Mongolian lamb

What a shame Mary Jane what a shame
Mary Jane had a pain at the party

All together now
What a shame Mary Jane had a pain at the party
What a shame what what a shame Mary
Jane had a pain at the party
What a shame what a shame what a shame what a shame

[That's it. Before we get taken away!]

STEP INSIDE LOVE 1996

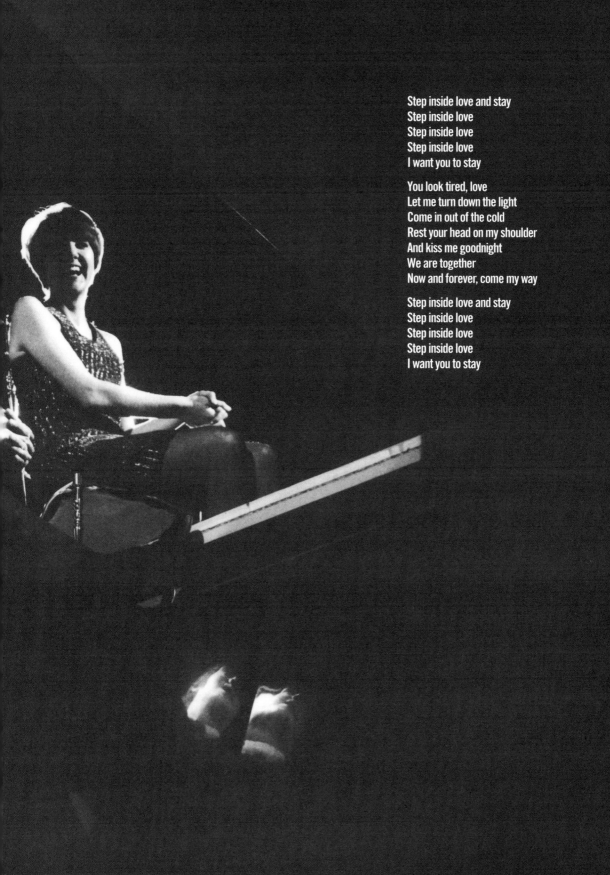

Step inside love and stay
Step inside love
Step inside love
Step inside love
I want you to stay

You look tired, love
Let me turn down the light
Come in out of the cold
Rest your head on my shoulder
And kiss me goodnight
We are together
Now and forever, come my way

Step inside love and stay
Step inside love
Step inside love
Step inside love
I want you to stay

TEDDY BOY
1996

This is the story
Of a boy named Ted
If his mother said
"Ted, be good (Be good, Ted)"
he would (alright)

She told him tales
About his soldier dad
But it made her sad
And she cried, oh my

Ted used to tell her
He'd be twice as good
And he knew he could
Cause in his head he said
"Mama don't worry
Your Teddy boy's here
Taking good care of you
Mama don't worry
Your Teddy boy's here
Teddy's gonna see you through"

And she said
"Teddy don't worry
Your Mama is here
Taking good care of you"
She said, "Teddy don't worry
Your mummy's here
Teddy's gonna see you through"

He said, "Ta da da…"

Then came the day
She found herself a man
Teddy turned and ran
Oh far away, oh yeah

He couldn't stand it
Just to be around
So he left the town far away
Yeah yeah

Ted used to tell her
He'd be twice as good
And he knew he could
Cause in his head he said
"Mama don't worry
Now Teddy boy's here
Taking good care of you
Mama don't worry
Your Teddy boy's here
Teddy's gonna see you through"

And she said
"Teddy don't worry
Now mummy is here
Taking good care of you
Teddy don't worry
Now your mummy's here
Mummy's gonna see you through"

And he said
"Mummy mummy don't worry
Your Teddy Boy's here
Taking good care of you
Mummy don't worry
Now Teddy Boy's here
Teddy's gonna see us through"

Take your partners
And dosi-do
Hold them tight
And don't let go
When you've got it. Jump up

Take your partners
And dosi-do
When you got it
Then let it go
Hold them tight and

Now Ted used to tell her
He'd be twice as good
And he knew he could
Cause in his head, he said

COME AND GET IT

1996

If you want it, here it is
Come and get it
Make your mind up fast
If you want it anytime I can give it
But you better hurry cause it may not last

Did I hear you say that there must be a catch?
Will you walk away from a fool and his money?

If you want it, here it is
Come and get it
But you better hurry cause it's going fast

If you want it, here it is
Come and get it
Make your mind up fast
If you want it anytime I can give it
But you'd better hurry cause it may not last

Did I hear you say that there must be a catch?
Will you walk away from a fool and his money?

Sonny, if you want it, here it is
Come and get it
But you'd better hurry cause it's going fast
You'd better hurry cause it's going fast

Woo, fool and his money

Sonny, if you want it, here it is
Come and get it
But you'd better hurry cause it's going fast
You'd better hurry cause it's going fast
You'd better hurry cause it's going fast

INDEX OF SONG TITLES

SONG CREDITS

I Saw Her Standing There Words and Music by John Lennon & Paul McCartney © 1963, Reproduced by permission of Sony/ATV Music Publishing (UK) Ltd/ Sony/ATV Tunes LLC, London W1F 9LD

Misery Words and Music by John Lennon & Paul McCartney © 1963, Reproduced by permission of Sony/ATV Music Publishing (UK) Ltd/ Sony/ATV Tunes LLC, London W1F 9LD

Do You Want To Know A Secret Words and Music by John Lennon & Paul McCartney © 1963, Reproduced by permission of Sony/ATV Music Publishing (UK) Ltd/ Sony/ATV Tunes LLC, London W1F 9LD

There's A Place Words and Music by John Lennon & Paul McCartney © 1963, Reproduced by permission of Sony/ATV Music Publishing (UK) Ltd/ Sony/ATV Tunes LLC, London W1F 9LD

From Me To You Words and Music by John Lennon & Paul McCartney © 1963. Reproduced by permission of Sony/ATV Music Publishing (UK) Ltd/ Sony/ATV Tunes LLC, London W1F 9LD

Thank You Girl Words and Music by John Lennon & Paul McCartney © 1963, Reproduced by permission of Sony/ATV Music Publishing (UK) Ltd/ Sony/ATV Tunes LLC, London W1F 9LD

She Loves You Words and Music by John Lennon & Paul McCartney © 1963, Reproduced by permission of Sony/ATV Music Publishing (UK) Ltd/ Sony/ATV Tunes LLC, London W1F 9LD

I'll Get You Words and Music by John Lennon & Paul McCartney © 1963, Reproduced by permission of Sony/ATV Music Publishing (UK) Ltd/ Sony/ATV Tunes LLC, London W1F 9LD

It Won't Be Long Words and Music by John Lennon & Paul McCartney © 1963. Reproduced by permission of Sony/ATV Music Publishing (UK) Ltd/ Sony/ATV Tunes LLC, London W1F 9LD

All I've Got To Do Words and Music by John Lennon & Paul McCartney © 1963. Reproduced by permission of Sony/ATV Music Publishing (UK) Ltd/ Sony/ATV Tunes LLC, London W1F 9LD

All My Loving Words and Music by John Lennon & Paul McCartney © 1963, Reproduced by permission of Sony/ATV Music Publishing (UK) Ltd/ Sony/ATV Tunes LLC, London W1F 9LD

Little Child Words and Music by John Lennon & Paul McCartney © 1963, Reproduced by permission of Sony/ATV Music Publishing (UK) Ltd/ Sony/ATV Tunes LLC, London W1F 9LD

Hold Me Tight Words and Music by John Lennon & Paul McCartney © 1963, Reproduced by permission of Sony/ATV Music Publishing (UK) Ltd/ Sony/ATV Tunes LLC, London W1F 9LD

Not A Second Time Words and Music by John Lennon & Paul McCartney © 1963, Reproduced by permission of Sony/ATV Music Publishing (UK) Ltd/ Sony/ATV Tunes LLC, London W1F 9LD

I Wanna Be Your Man Words and Music by John Lennon & Paul McCartney © 1963, Reproduced by permission of Sony/ATV Music Publishing (UK) Ltd/ Sony/ATV Tunes LLC, London W1F 9LD

This Boy Words and Music by John Lennon & Paul McCartney © 1963, Reproduced by permission of Sony/ATV Music Publishing (UK) Ltd/ Sony/ATV Tunes LLC, London W1F 9LD

I Call Your Name Words and Music by John Lennon & Paul McCartney © 1963. Reproduced by permission of Sony/ATV Music Publishing (UK) Ltd/ Sony/ATV Tunes LLC, London W1F 9LD

A Hard Day's Night Words and Music by John Lennon & Paul McCartney © 1964, Reproduced by permission of Sony/ATV Music Publishing (UK) Ltd/ Sony/ATV Tunes LLC, London W1F 9LD

I Should Have Known Better Words and Music by John Lennon & Paul McCartney © 1964, Reproduced by permission of Sony/ATV Music Publishing (UK) Ltd/ Sony/ATV Tunes LLC, London W1F 9LD

If I Fell Words and Music by John Lennon & Paul McCartney © 1964, Reproduced by permission of Sony/ATV Music Publishing (UK) Ltd/ Sony/ATV Tunes LLC, London W1F 9LD

And I Love Her Words and Music by John Lennon & Paul McCartney © 1963, Reproduced by permission of Sony/ATV Music Publishing (UK) Ltd/ Sony/ATV Tunes LLC, London W1F 9LD

I'm Happy Just To Dance With You Words and Music by John Lennon & Paul McCartney © 1964, Reproduced by permission of Sony/ATV Music Publishing (UK) Ltd/ Sony/ATV Tunes LLC, London W1F 9LD

Tell Me Why Words and Music by John Lennon & Paul McCartney © 1964, Reproduced by permission of Sony/ATV Music Publishing (UK) Ltd/ Sony/ATV Tunes LLC, London W1F 9LD

Can't Buy Me Love Words and Music by John Lennon & Paul McCartney © 1964, Reproduced by permission of Sony/ATV Music Publishing (UK) Ltd/ Sony/ATV Tunes LLC, London W1F 9LD

Any Time At All Words and Music by John Lennon & Paul McCartney © 1964, Reproduced by permission of Sony/ATV Music Publishing (UK) Ltd/ Sony/ATV Tunes LLC, London W1F 9LD

I'll Cry Instead Words and Music by John Lennon & Paul McCartney © 1964, Reproduced by permission of Sony/ATV Music Publishing (UK) Ltd/ Sony/ATV Tunes LLC, London W1F 9LD

Things We Said Today Words and Music by John Lennon & Paul McCartney © 1964, Reproduced by permission of Sony/ATV Music Publishing (UK) Ltd/ Sony/ATV Tunes LLC, London W1F 9LD

When I Get Home Words and Music by John Lennon & Paul McCartney © 1964. Reproduced by permission of Sony/ATV Music Publishing (UK) Ltd/ Sony/ATV Tunes LLC, London W1F 9LD

You Can't Do That Words and Music by John Lennon & Paul McCartney © 1964. Reproduced by permission of Sony/ATV Music Publishing (UK) Ltd/ Sony/ATV Tunes LLC, London W1F 9LD

I'll Be Back Words and Music by John Lennon & Paul McCartney © 1964, Reproduced by permission of Sony/ATV Music Publishing (UK) Ltd/ Sony/ATV Tunes LLC, London W1F 9LD

I Feel Fine Words and Music by John Lennon & Paul McCartney © 1964, Reproduced by permission of Sony/ATV Music Publishing (UK) Ltd/ Sony/ATV Tunes LLC, London W1F 9LD

She's A Woman Words and Music by John Lennon & Paul McCartney © 1964, Reproduced by permission of Sony/ATV Music Publishing (UK) Ltd/ Sony/ATV Tunes LLC, London W1F 9LD

Eight Days A Week Words and Music by John Lennon & Paul McCartney © 1964, Reproduced by permission of Sony/ATV Music Publishing (UK) Ltd/ Sony/ATV Tunes LLC, London W1F 9LD

I'm A Loser Words and Music by John Lennon & Paul McCartney © 1964, Reproduced by permission of Sony/ATV Music Publishing (UK) Ltd/ Sony/ATV Tunes LLC, London W1F 9LD

PICTURE CREDITS

The publishers would like to thank the following sources for their kind permission to reproduce the pictures in this book.

Alamy: Archivio GBB 203; /Michael Burrell 154; /Chronicle 195; /Pump Park Vintage Photography 189; /Everett Collection 153; /Mike Greenslade 164l;/Alistair Laming 161b; /David Litschel 200-201;/MediaPunch 78-79; /Mirrorpix 90-91, 158, 158 (inset) 162-163, 175, 204, 238-239; /Malcolm Park 70-71; /Photo 12 86-87; /Sueddeutsche Zeitung Photo 194; /TCD.Prod.DB 280; /Tracks Images 16, 39, 274; /Ivan Vdovin 164b

Camera Press, London: Photograph by Terence Spencer: 9

© DMG Media Licensing: 148-149

Getty Images: Fiona Adams/Redferns 14, 42; /Dick Barnatt/Redferns 262; /Bentley Archive/Popperfoto 85; /Bettmann 74, 109, 241, 242, 293; /Blank Archives 46-47; /Christies 265; /Jim Dyson 138; /Larry Ellis/Daily Express/Hulton Archive 58; /Evening Standard 88; /Express 236-237; /Express/Archive Photos 246; /Godong/Universal Images Group 178; /GraphicaArtis 213; /Jim Gray/Keystone 243; /Harry Hammond/V&A Images 26; /Koh Hasebe/Shinko Music 220-221, 222; /Mark and Colleen Hayward/Redferns 17, 32, 61, 72-73, 119, 141, 278-279; /Jeff Hochberg 223; /Jim Hughes/NY Daily News Archive 81; /Hulton Archive 33, 184, 196-197, 290-291; /Hulton-Deutsch Collection/CORBIS 10-11, 12-13, 29, 94-95, 263; /Kaye/Daily Express/Hulton Archive 60; /Kelso/Liverpool Echo/Mirrorpix 149; /Keystone 21, 36, 108, 143, 250-251; /Keystone-France/Gamma-Rapho 40-41, 177, 205; /Tom King/Mirrorpix 260; /Les Lee/Daily Express/Hulton Archive 187; /The LIFE Picture Collection 270; /LMPC 124-125, 228; /John Loengard/The LIFE Picture Collection 106; /William Lovelace/Express 59; /LMPC 20, 68; /C. Maher/Daily Express/Hulton Archive 231; /Fred W. McDarrah 182-183; /Daily Herald/Mirrorpix 76-77; /Daily Mirror/Mirrorpix 50, 52, 53, 103, 132-133, 188; /Michael Ochs Archives 22-23, 54-55, 65, 268-269, 277, 288; 289; /Mike Mitchell/Paul Popper/Popperfoto 18-19, 63, 75; /Chris Morphet/Redferns 30-31; /Terry O'Neill/Iconic Images 212; /Gianni Penati/Condé Nast 83; /Jan Persson/Redferns 190-191; /George Peters 151; /Popperfoto 100-101; /Spot-Trond Topstad 192-193; /Sunday People/Mirrorpix 118, 244-245; /Potter/Express 166; /John Pratt/Keystone/Hulton Archive 120-121, 160-161; /RB 227, 235; /SSPL 167; /George Stroud/Express 134; /Art Zelin 207; /Stan Wayman/The LIFE Picture Collection 25; /Robert Whitaker 85, 90, 112-113, 128, 208-209, 286-287, 294-295; /Frederick Wilfred 234; /Brian Rasic 254-255; / Val Wilmer/Redferns 275; / Max Scheler – K&K endpapers.

Mirrorpix: 27, 266-267

NASA: 252

Photo12: Jean Marie-Periér 304

Public Domain: 150

Runner1928 via Wikimedia Commons 198-199

Shutterstock Editorial: AP 43, 49, 80, 130, 281; /Bob Dear/AP 202; /Bournemouth News 67, 180, 277; /Matt Cetti-Roberts/Lnp 122-123; /Daily Mail 104; /Granger 34; /Dezo Hoffman 35; /Julien's Auctions 44; /David Magnus 172, 173; /Moviestore 290-291; /Paul Felix 232;

Unsplash: John Matychuk 105

All other illustrations provided by Shutterstock

Every effort has been made to acknowledge correctly and contact the source and/or copyright holder of each picture and Welbeck Publishing apologises for any unintentional errors or omissions, which will be corrected in future editions of this book.